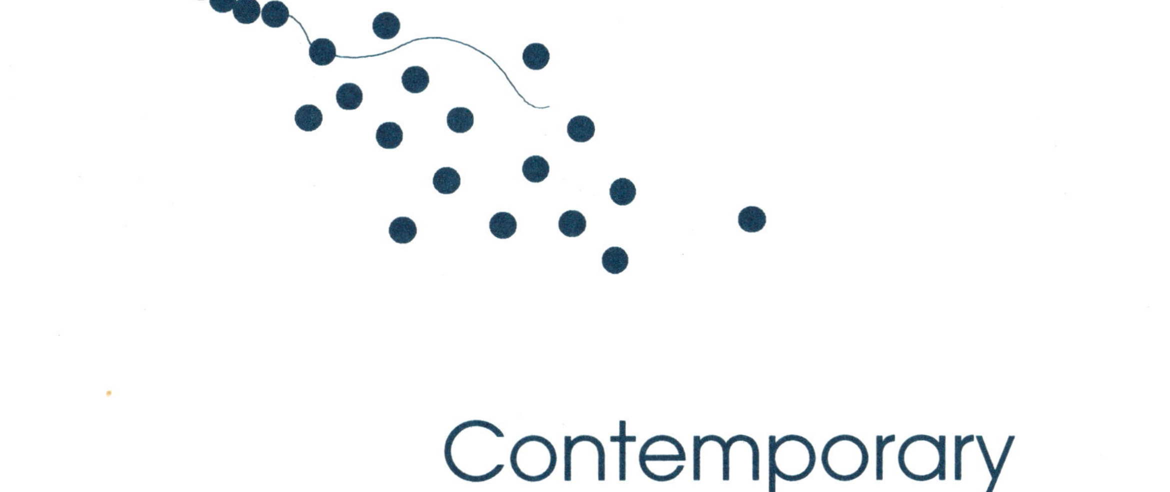

Contemporary Beadwork I:
Counted and Charted Patterns
for Flat Peyote Stitch

by Diane Fitzgerald

Published by
Beautiful Beads Press
115 Hennepin Avenue
Minneapolis, MN 55401
612-333-0170
Fax: 612-333-8122

*This book is dedicated
to
my husband, Alan Shilepsky,
without his encouragement and computers
this book would not have been possible;
to
my mother, Adeline Farmer,
whose dedication to counted crosstitch
inspired me to write this book;
and to
my grandchildren, Adam, Scott and Kaitlin,
who continually renew my energy and outlook on life.*

Special thanks to Elaine Clelland, Mary Klotz, Louise Sakellaris, Billie Jacobs and Barbara Brown for their help and/or advice.

Table of Contents

About the Author

Diane Fitzgerald is a bead artist who works in a variety of contemporary bead assemblage techniques. This includes what is traditionally considered beadwork using seed beads, and bead assemblage with larger beads. Since 1989, she has taught an eclectic variety of bead classes at her shop, Beautiful Beads, in Minneapolis, Minnesota and around the country. As a bead collector, she specializes in contemporary art glass beads, particularly American, European and Japanese. Recently, she visited the Czech Republic and Germany to learn about the glass bead industry and meet beadmakers there. Diane is co-author with Helen Banes of "Beads and Threads: A New Technique for Fiber Jewelry," published by Flower Valley Press. She is the founder of the Upper Midwest Bead Society and her work has been exhibited in several shows.

About This Book

I hope you enjoy this book at least half as much as I enjoyed writing it. If you do, it will give you an immense amount of pleasure. In writing it and developing the patterns, I would often become so engrossed in it that I would be at my computer for 12-14 hours a day. The potential for peyote stitch patterns is limitless and now, with the Bead-Line Guide and the Bead-Line Graph Paper, following charted peyote patterns has been simplified. I hope you find that the system I've developed works for you. Please take time to read the text before starting a pattern so you will understand how the written bead counts work as well as many other facets of the peyote stitch. I would be delighted to see photos of your work, help with problems, receive feedback or just to visit. If you are in Minneapolis, please stop by my shop, Beautiful Beads, at 115 Hennepin Avenue.

The Universal Bead

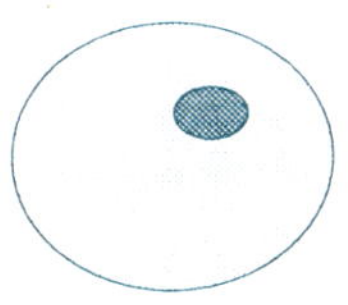

It may start with just a few beads. As a child they enticed you with their color or reflected light. Maybe your grandmother gave you a special string of wonderful old glass beads. Some strands might be broken but you've saved them in a little box tucked away in a drawer.

If you grew up in another culture, you may have a rich heritage of beadwork which embellished both everyday items and those for special occasions.

Maybe somewhere among your ancestors, there was a bead trader, or a traveler who picked up beads and carried them along the great trade routes of the world.

Further back, there may have been someone who found a brightly colored stone or shell and, for good luck, found a way to pierce it and wear it as an adornment. Beads are universal in their appeal and have been so since human beings first began to clothe themselves. They have served to mark our prayers and our special occasions and have played a role in land deals and love affairs.

Wear your beads with pride. They are miniature works of art meant for everyone to enjoy!

Some Background on Seed Beads

When you work with these tiny beads, you join a 500-year tradition which spans most continents and even more cultures. European explorers traded colorful glass beads with their hosts in Africa and the New World enabling the recipients to embellish their garments and other items with a less labor-intensive decoration than they had used previously. Native Americans applied beads to their clothing and wove beads into belts, armbands and headdresses. Africans, such as the Ndebele, relied on beaded adornments to indicate passage to new phases of life such as adolescence and marriage. In Indonesia, baby carriers and baskets were covered with beads and often indicated status. Today, American artists use seed beads the way artists use oil paints, as a means of self-expression.

In the early 1990s, seed beads were made in seven countries. The Czech Republic lead in output with 2,300 tons. They also make the tiniest beads, 1.2 mm. India and Taiwan were the next largest producers at 1,400 tons each per year. Japan followed with 1,200 tons; Italy at 920 tons; France, 120 tons and last, Austria with 80 tons. (Newsletter of the Bead Society of Greater Washington, Feb./ Mar., 1990)

Seed beads have been produced in Italy and the Czech Republic (formerly Czechoslovakia), also known as Bohemia, for hundreds of years. Glass seed beads, sometimes referred to by their French name, rocaille, are made by the "drawn" method of working glass, one of five methods which include blowing, molding, winding (lampwork) and fusing. The drawn method involves taking a molten glob of glass, into which a bubble of air has been blown, and pulling it into a long hollow tube, usually about 300 feet long! The air bubble becomes the hole in the bead. The tube is cut into pieces which become the seed beads or bugle beads. The beads are then tumbled with clay-like material and heated and tumbled some more to slightly melt and round off the sharp edges. Further shaking after the beads cool causes the clay to fall out. Finally the beads are sorted by size. Because the holes in bugle beads are long, the holes cannot be filled with clay to prevent collapse. As a result, these beads are not tumbled and their edges are sharp. Beware that they can cut your thread!

Glass beads are made from sand and metals. The addition of different metals results in different colors, such as cobalt (blue), copper (blue, red, pink and brown), chromium (green), cadmium (yellow), silver (amber), manganese (violet and pink with a brownish tinge), selenium (red, orange), and gold (ruby red and pink). Adding fluorine, tin or phosphate changes the transparency of glass to opaque or opalescent. A semi-transparent glass is known as "greasy" glass because it resembles petroleum jelly.

Various color effects can be achieved in a variety of ways. Finishes on the outside of the beads can change their color.

Types of finishes include iridescent (sometimes called carnival, rainbow or AB for aurora borealis), luster, gold-washed, galvanized (metallic, a finish which may rub off), dyed (the color may change) and pearlized. The appearance can also be changed by applying paint or other finishes to the inside of the bead hole. Examples are silver-lined, gold-lined or color-lined beads. Unusual effects are achieved by applying color inside colored transparent beads such as a transparent blue glass lined with violet paint. Another effect on color results from use of satin glass(a striated finish). You can affect the color by mixing two or more colors of beads together or by using different colors of thread.

Shapes can vary as well. Beads may be round, facetted or square-cut on the ends (two-cuts). Beads with many facets are called three-cuts beads and beads with only one facet are called charlottes. Charlottes are highly prized by some because they are somewhat hard to find and because they give a very subtle sparkle to your work.

Beads may be sold strung in hanks or by weight in tubes or bags. Japanese beads and other non-European seed beads are usually sold by the gram or kilo while Czech beads are sold strung by the hank. A hank consists of 10-14 strands, each 12-14 inches in length. (Older hanks of beads may be only 4-6 inches in length.) One hank is approximately an ounce, the same as some tubes of beads. Buying beads by weight may result in a differing number of actual beads per ounce because the size of the hole may vary, thus there may be more or less weight per bead.

Bead sizes generally range from size 5 to size 18, but may go to as small as size 24. Sizes of beads are noted as 11/0 or 11°; the higher the number the smaller the bead. This is read as eleven ought, size eleven or simply elevens. The most common bead size used today is size 11 although new supplies of size 14 beads from Japan may make this size nearly as popular. Like shoes, there may be a wide range of actual sizes of beads within one size. Japanese beads seem to be the most uniform and consistent in size. As in most projects, try to obtain all the beads needed for one project, and preferably from one manufacturer, before you start. Bead supplies can be erratic. The general rule is, if you see beads you like, buy as many as you can afford. You may never see those beads again. (Advice offered by Virginia Blakelock.)

Storing your beads:
There are many ways to store your beads, but perhaps the most popular are the small reclosable plastic bags or plastic tubes. Some prefer to use clear plastic boxes that are 2" x 2" x 3/4".

These bags and tubes can be stored in other plastics bags, boxes or various types of holders. I use plastic bags and store them in several 60-drawer plastic cabinets available in hardware stores. I sort them in sections by color. Hardware and fishing departments are good places to find plastic boxes but don't overlook the cosmetic, drug or children's sections of your local discount stores.

Bead Sizes:
Seed beads are generally less than 2 mm in size. There are about 17-19 size 11 beads to the inch.

Beadwork Basics

There are many ways of assembling beads. In addition to simply stringing, beads may be woven, knitted, crocheted, knotted, braided, embroidered, netted, laced, set in wax or glued to create or embellish a surface. The basic tools described below will help you get started with many of these techniques.

The Basic Tool Kit for Beaders
Have Bead Kit — Will Travel

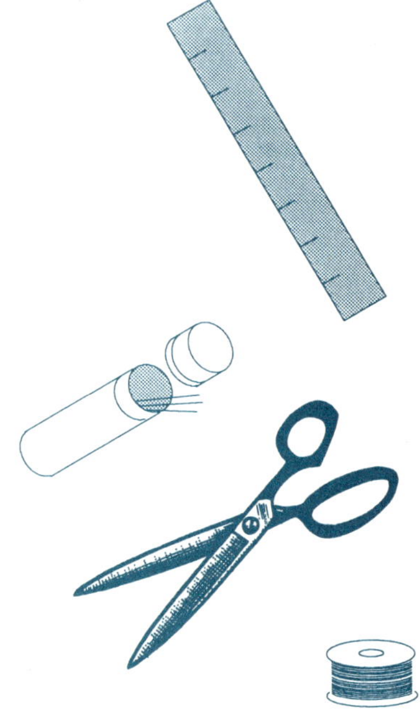

Do bead work in a car or when traveling? Why not? I have my beadwork tools in a small plastic box ready to slip into my purse at a moment's notice. Here's what it contains:
- small sharp scissor
- several needles in a needle holder
- a spool each of black and white Nymo D thread on the spool and bobbins in several colors
- fresh clear nail polish
- lighter
- 5-inch ruler
- beeswax
- small dishes
- "gripper"

This last item, the gripper, may be a hemostat, a surgical gripping tool, or a tweezers which opens and closes like a scissor. I find it very helpful in easing the needle through some tight holes. Sometimes even a small piece of thin rubbery material or leather will help grip the needle and ease it through. Pull gently but firmly without bending the needle.

Needles

Most beading needles are made in England or Japan. In English sizes, size 16 is the smallest and in Japanese, size 16 is the largest. The Japanese needles are very stiff while the English needles will bend instead of break. For most off-loom work where I pick up only one or a few beads at a time, I prefer the size 12 English needles which are called "Sharps." These needles are about 1 1/4" long. They are less expensive and bend less easily than beading needles. Size 12 needles will go through most beads as small as size 14, depending on the size of thread used and the beads. Nymo D thread (see below) will go through a size 12 needle. For loomwork, scooping or long strands of beads, I use an English beading needle.

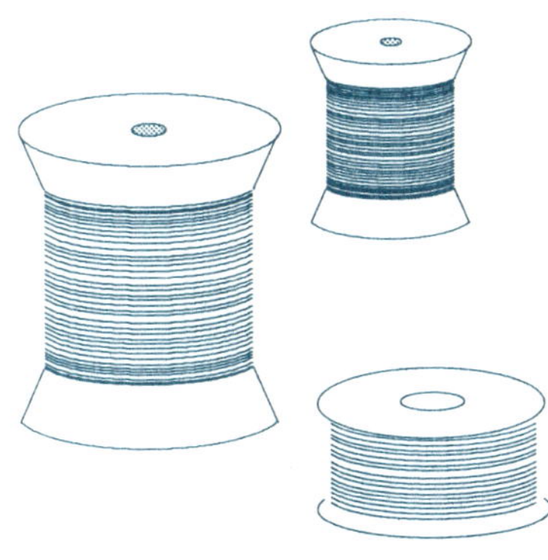

Thread

My favorite thread, Nymo D, is made by the Belding-Hemmingway Company which has been making thread for more than 150 years. It is a monocord nylon thread, which means it is made of several monofilaments. It is very tough and durable. It is available on a bobbin which has 80 yards or on a spool which has 300 yards. Bobbins are sometimes available in a variety of colors while the spools come in only black or white. If you're really into beading, get a cone which has four times the thread on a spool and you'll be set with a near-lifetime supply. Note: cones come only in white, and the thread is just like that on the spool.

Nymo thread comes in several weights: D is the heaviest, B is medium and A or 00 is the finest. Size F is also available and is slightly heavier than D, but I seldom use it because it is too thick when multiple strands must fit in a bead hole.

If you compare Nymo D on the spool and on the bobbin, you'll notice a difference. The thread on the bobbin is softer than the thread on the spool. This gets back to the purpose for which this thread is manufactured: the shoe and leather industry. Shoes and purses are assembled on sewing machines which have a spool to feed thread to the needle and a bobbin to feed thread up from the bottom. The Nymo thread on the spool is made to feed the needle and so it is called a "needle" thread. Because it feeds through the needle, it must be slightly stronger and it is given a silicon coating to lubricate it as it passes through the needle. The thread on the bobbins are somewhat lighter weight and are coated with a slightly tacky substance to keep them from unraveling from the bobbin.

Weight or tensile strength of Nymo thread (breaking point when weight is placed on the thread)

	Spool thread	Bobbin thread
D	8.2 lbs	5.7
B	4.5	4.2
A	4.1	4.0
00	2.2	2.1

The bottom line: if you want a softer feel to your bead-work, use the lighter weight thread on the bobbin. If you want durability, use a heavier weight thread on the spool.

An alternative to Nymo thread is Silamide Waxed Thread for Hand Sewing, Size A, made by the A. H. Rice Company of Pittsfield, Massachusetts. It is a thread used by tailors and is available in a range of colors. Since it is a twisted thread, it may be a little harder to thread it into the needle, but its twist is also its benefit. For sculptural projects where you want tight tension, pull it tight and it will hold the beads in the shape you wish. The wax helps hold the tension as well. The twisted thread also enables you to do twisted fringe. There are 675 yards per package. The A. H. Rice Company has recently begun to make a thread very similar to Nymo. Their thread is called Nylmo.

A second alternative that some people swear by is Kevlar, the thread of which bullet-proof vests are made. It is available in several colors and is very strong and fine.

Light Up Your Life

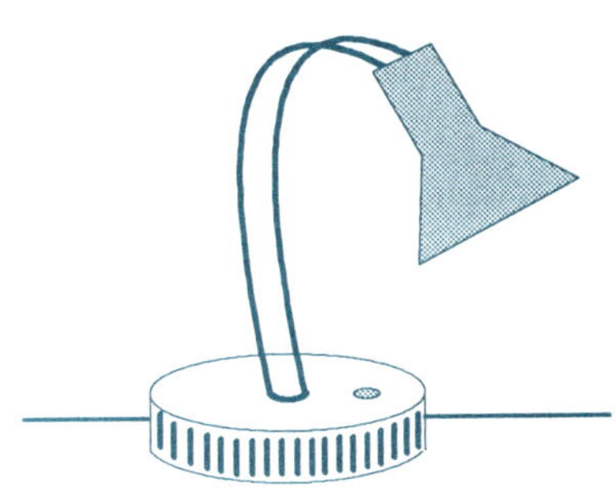

Good light is an absolute must when doing beadwork, especially as you get older. If you can't see the beads, the bead holes and the needle hole, you just may need a little help. You may need to have your eyes checked or try the half-glasses that sit on the end of your nose for reading. A magnifying glass that rests on your chest and is supported by a cord can also be a big help. Special lamps which have a circular fluorescent bulb or incandescent bulb and a magnifying glass are great. These may be free-standing or clamp-on and have a flexible arm so you can put it exactly where you need it.

When I work at my desk, I have two flexible-arm lamps with 60- or 100-watt bulbs shining on my work from both right and left at a 45-degree angle. I also rely on overhead or ambient light. Bouncing the light from the new halogen floor lamps off the ceiling can light a room up like daylight. Remember, the type of light used will affect how you see the color of your beads. I prefer incandescent light.

Peyote Stitch Patterns

The peyote stitch is a popular off-loom beading technique used to create a "cloth of beads." It is done by adding one or more beads at a time using a needle and thread. Many people find it a relaxing and fulfilling artform.

Just as in learning any new skill, producing a pattern in peyote stitch can be challenging at first. However, once you understand how the beads lie in relation to each other and how each row is added, designs can be charted on graph paper and counted, much like counted cross-stitch, needlepoint or knitting. The difference is that in these types of stitchery the graph used is a simple grid of boxes placed in vertical columns and horizontal rows (Fig. 2). Peyote stitch shares the vertical columns with these needlearts. However, instead of horizontal rows, each row is offset so the beads appear to lie in diagonal lines. These diagonal lines are at an approximately 45 degree angle to the vertical columns of beads, forming a brick-like pattern, as shown in Fig. 1.

Certain shapes can be made more easily with one type of graph than the other. The ordinary horizontal-vertical graph is good for making squares, rectangles and straight lines both horizontally and vertically. With the peyote stitch graph, you can make triangles, hexagons, rhombuses and straight vertical or diagonal lines (Fig. 3). (You can make other shapes with both kinds of graphing patterns, they just won't be as precise.) These simple shapes can be combined in an infinite number of ways to create wonderful patterns, including quilting motifs such as Texas Star, line motifs such as Celtic knots, interlaced Islamic patterns and geometric shapes that create optical illusions such as the Tumbling Blocks. Have fun exploring these shapes using the graph paper included in this book.

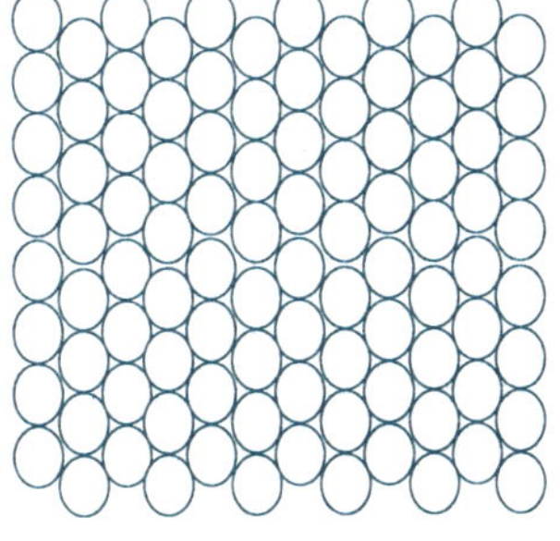

Fig. 1. Diagonal-vertical graphing pattern for peyote stitch

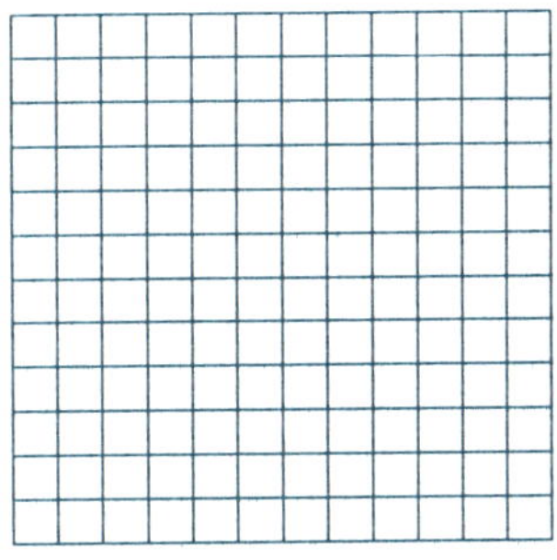

Fig. 2. Ordinary horizontal-vertical graph pattern for counted cross stitch, needlepoint and other needlearts.

Fig. 3

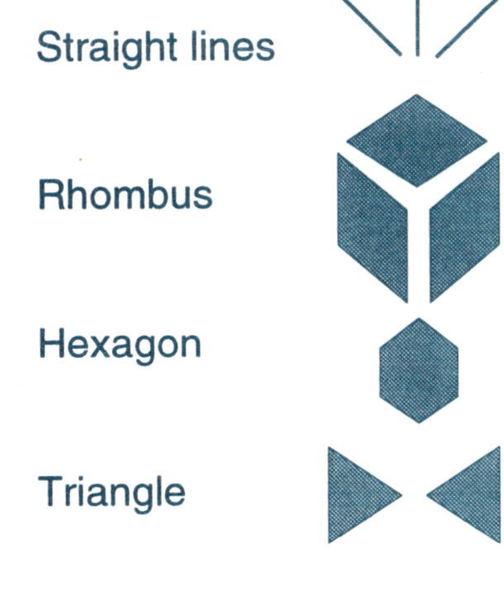

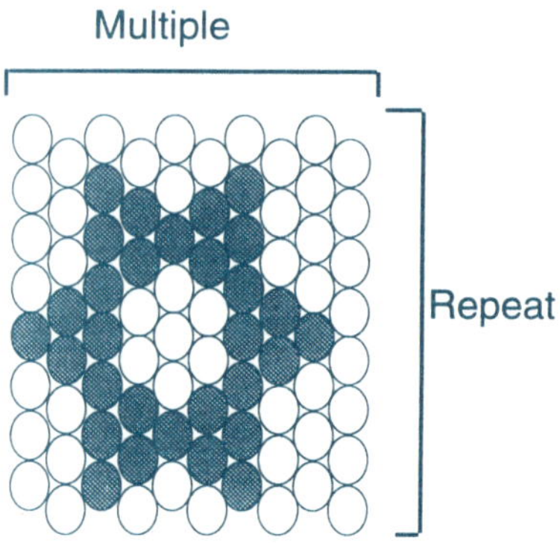

How to Read Patterns in This Book

Terms

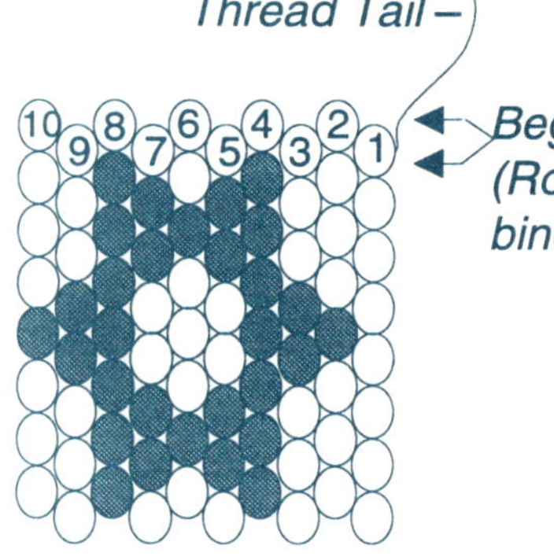

Fig. 4

Multiple: defines the <u>width</u> of one unit of the design and equals the number of beads in two rows. The Multiple also refers to the number of beads strung on in the Beginning Row.

Repeat refers to the number of rows of beads in the <u>length</u> of one unit of the design.

Row: Each row across has half the number of beads specified in the multiple. This is because each row of peyote stitch adds only every other bead. The following row fills in the spaces between the beads.

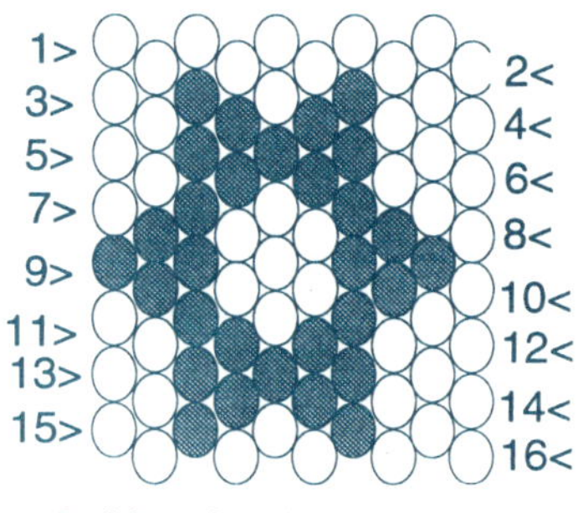

Fig. 5

Reading a Pattern

The **"Beginning Row"** is counted from right to left and <u>includes the first two rows.</u> Counting the Beginning Row from right to left enables you to begin work from left to right with Row 3. For example, in the diagram at the left, Fig. 5, the Beginning Row has ten light beads (Its multiple is 10). Bead colors are indicated by L= Light, M = Medium, D = Dark.

Row 3, as shown in Fig. 6, is worked from left to right. Row 3 would be written:
Row 3> 1L, 1D, 1L, 1D, 1L

and Row 4, Fig. 6, is worked from right to left. It would be written:

Row 4< 2L, 2D, 1L

The arrows (<>) in the written bead counts shown for each row indicate the direction in which the row is worked. For example, Row 5>, indicates that row is worked left to right. Remember to keep your thread tail in the upper right hand corner of your work.

Fig. 6 shows how rows are numbered, odd numbers on the left and even numbers on the right.

<u>Note:</u> When looking at the right side of your work, the thread tail will be in the upper right hand corner.

Fig. 6. Numbering rows in peyote stitch

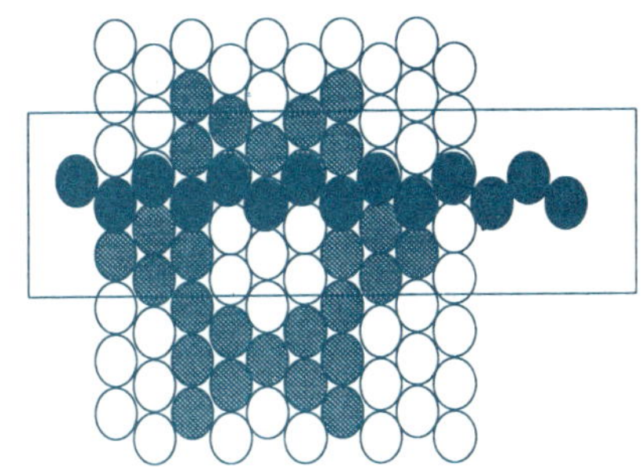

Fig. 7 The Bead-Line Guide laid over a graphed pattern.

Note: Two Bead-Line Guides are provided with this book. They are located on the page with the Bead-Line Graph Transparency at the back of this book. A sample is also shown below.

Using the Bead-Line Guide

Working from a graphed peyote pattern is easy using the Bead-Line Guide and the Bead-Line Graph Paper included with this book. The Bead-Line Guide (shown on page 14) is a clear piece of acetate that has a row of solid color bead shapes printed on it which match the bead grid on the charts. The Bead-Line Guide is designed to provide a clear guide to exactly which beads are in a row. It is placed just below the row on which you are working and is shifted to the right or left by one row as you work down the pattern. You may hold the Bead-Line Guide in place with a piece of easily removable tape; tape it to a magnetic ruler and use it with an upright sheet holder such as secretaries or embroiderers use; or glue or tape it to a clear plastic ruler to hold it in place.

The Bead-Line Graph Paper has been designed to work with the Bead-Line Guide. It has large, clear ovals to represent beads. With large, distinct ovals, you can see each bead on the graph paper making it easy to count the number of beads.These ovals are approximately four times the size of a size 11 bead. As a result, if you used size 11 beads your finished piece would be half as wide and half as long as your graphed version. Each pattern is shown full size in the upper right corner of the page. The pattern is also shown repeated one or more times and reduced to represent size 11 beads. The graph paper in this book may be purchased from Beautiful Beads or you may copy it for your individual use only. It may not be copied for use in classes or for sale.

1. Using a Bead-Line Guide: There are several ways to use the Bead-Line Guide. If you are working with a pattern that is a drawing, a free-form design, a very large pattern or one that does not repeat very often, you may wish to use the Bead-Line Guide and read the pattern directly from the graph, similar to the way knitters and cross-stitchers do without writing down each bead in the row.

You may find it helpful to color your pattern with colored pencils or fine-point marking pens. If you make a mistake on your pattern, you may be able to erase it or use correction fluid. If not, just cut out the error and inset a clean piece of graph paper from the back, holding it in place with tape.

The Bead-Line Guide

To work from a free-form colored design, lay a transparent copy of the Bead-Line Graph Paper over your design, then have it copied on a color copier. Use the Bead-Line Guide as described above.

2. Written Bead Counts: For smaller, simpler patterns that repeat horizontally and vertically, you may wish to count the sequence of beads in each row and write them down, just as I have done for you in the patterns shown in this book. Use the Bead-Line-Guide to indicate the row and write down each bead as it occurs in the row. For example, Row 37> 3 red, 4 blue, 2 green, etc. Note: The bead counts in parentheses should be repeated according to the number which follows. For example a count that is written, (1L, 2D) x 2, would be repeated twice: 1Light, 2Dark, 1Light, 2Dark.

Using Patterns in Your Beadwork

You may use the patterns included in this book in a number of ways. For some of your projects, you may wish to change the width of the pattern. The width of each pattern as shown is indicated by the Multiple which tells how many beads are across the Beginning Row. To make a pattern wider, you may double it, that is, repeat the Beginning Row as many times as needed to create the width of the piece you need. You may also simply add a solid color border of two, four or any even number of beads on one or both sides. Combining two or more patterns is another option. Drawing out a full-color chart with pens, pencils, crayons or markers is always a good idea so that you can see how your ideas will look and to have a chart to follow.

Check Your Work!

Save yourself frustration. Take the time to compare your just completed row with the pattern. This saves lots of ripping.

Hint: If you have trouble with beads twisting when you begin your first few rows of peyote stitich, it might be helpful to do the first four rows in a solid color, then begin the pattern with Row 1. (Row 1 will be at the end of the counted instructions.)Later, you can remove these extra rows.

How To Do Flat Peyote Stitch

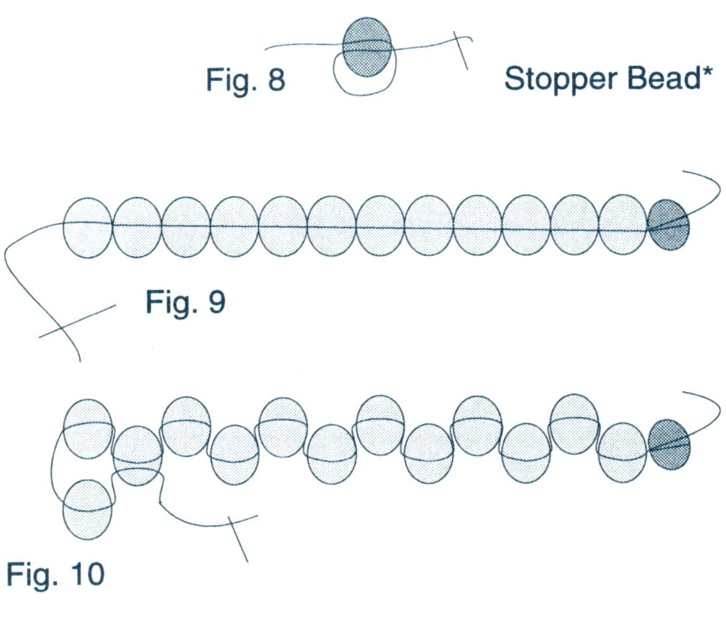

Fig. 8 — Stopper Bead*

Fig. 9

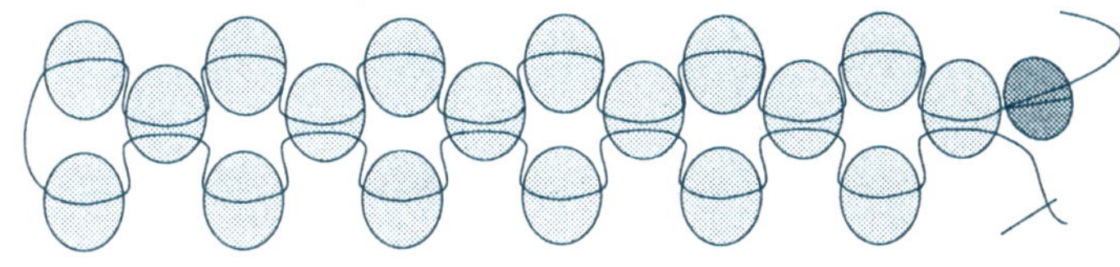

Fig. 10

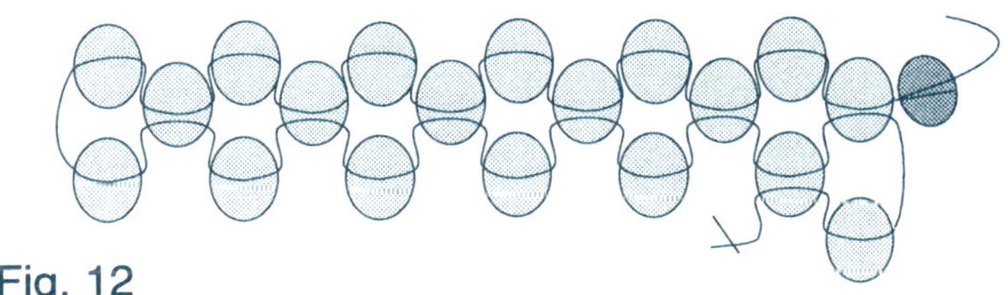

Fig. 11

Fig. 12

*The darker shaded bead in each row is the Stopper Bead.

1. Thread your needle with a 36" piece of thread. Don't knot the thread. String on a "stopper" bead which will later be removed. Go through the stopper bead a second time in the same direction, being careful not to pierce the thread (Fig. 8). Leave a 4-6" tail.

2. String on the beads according to the Beginning Row of your pattern (Fig. 9).

3. Pick up the first bead of Row 1 and go into the second bead from the end of the Beginning Row (Fig. 10).

4. Pick up the second bead of Row 1 and go into the fourth bead from the end of the Beginning Row. After adding each bead, push the beads tightly together so that they begin to form a brick-like pattern as shown at left (Fig. 11). Keep your thread tight.

5. Continue to pick up one bead at a time following the colors indicated by the pattern and, working in the same direction, pass your needle into the second bead counting from the one you just left.

6. At the end of the row, add the first bead of the new row, turn your work and go into the last bead of the previous row (Fig. 12). (Do not go through the stopper bead.)

Note: It is especially important to avoid piercing the thread already in the bead for two reasons: first, the thread will wear out faster as the beadwork moves; second, the first row is usually a little tight but can be loosened if the threads haven't been sewn together.

Hint: As I work, I hold the piece in my left hand between my thumb and index finger. I wrap the working thread over the side of my index finger and hold it tight with my middle finger. Think of it as a finger and bead sandwich, your middle finger is a slice of bread, your index finger is baloney, the beads are the mustard and your thumb is the bottom piece of bread. Hmm. . . makes me hungry!

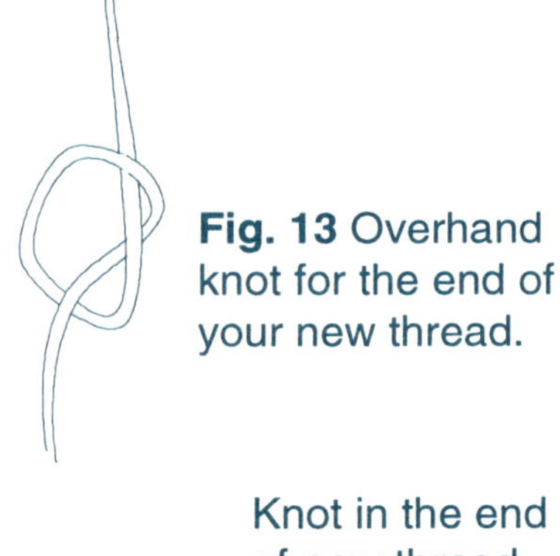

Fig. 13 Overhand knot for the end of your new thread.

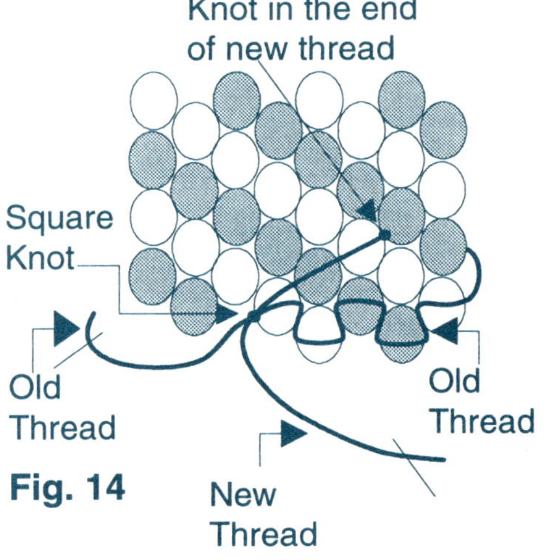

Knot in the end of new thread

Square Knot

Old Thread

Old Thread

Fig. 14

New Thread

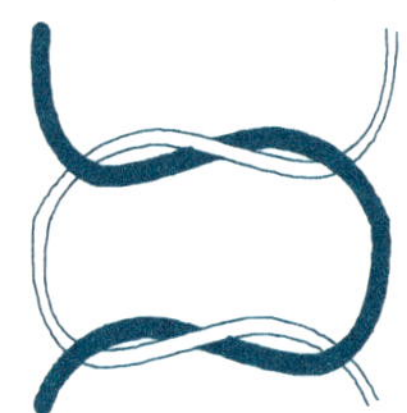

Fig. 15. Square Knot: Left thread goes over the right thread and around it. Then the right thread goes over the left thread and passes through the loop.

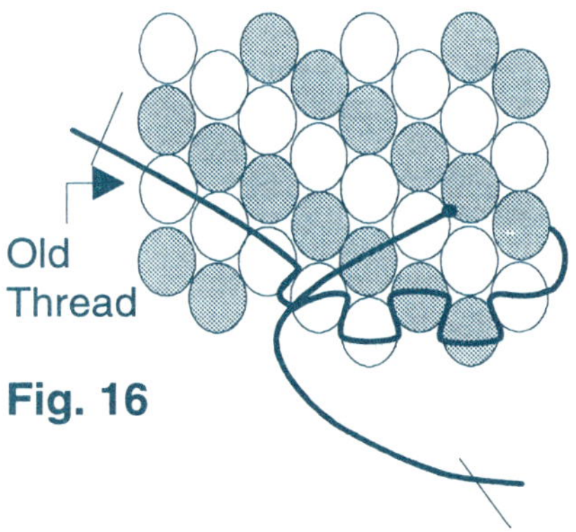

Old Thread

Fig. 16

Tying On A New Thread

I use the two-needle method of tying on a new thread. I don't like to have loose ends hanging from my work and I like a secure knot. In fact, with this method, you have two knots, for those of us who want our work to last a hundred years, at least!

When your present thread is worked down to about three to four inches, it's time to tie on a new thread.

Leave the needle on the old thread. Thread a new needle and put an overhand knot in the end (Fig. 13). Cut the tail off close to the knot (1/16th inch) and melt it with a lighter or dab clear fingernail polish on it. When melting the knot, put the end of the thread near the base of the flame where it is the hottest and flickers the least. It is not necessary to put the knot in the flame. Always test the knot to be sure it holds by pulling on it.

Bring the new thread through three or four beads of the existing work so that the thread comes out of the <u>same bead hole</u> as the old thread and <u>in the same direction</u>. The knot should be buried in a bead (Fig. 14). Tie the old thread to the new thread with a <u>square knot</u> (Fig. 15). Bring the old thread (with the needle still on it) through three to four beads (Fig. 16). Pull tightly so the knot is buried in the bead hole if possible. Clip off the remaining thread close to the beads. Put a dot of clear nail polish on the knot. If your knot shows, touch it up with a matching marking pen before applying the nail polish. You're all set to continue beading.

Beadwork Embellishment Ideas

If you're not already an avid beadworker, you may be wondering how you can use these patterns. Here are just a few ideas:

Bracelet
Basket
Choker
Necklace
Earrings
Edgings and Trims
Chains or Straps
Pocket Flap
Pocket
Collar
Flat Purse or Clutch Purse
Charm Bag or Medicine Pouch
Draw String Purse
Coin Purse
Eye Glass Case
Belt
Hat Band
Cuff
Sandals or slippers
Book Cover
Picture frame
Placemat
Coaster
Men's tie
Wallhanging
Pillow Cover
Pen Holder
Eye Glass Case
Switch Plate Cover
Insulator Tube for Windows
Plant Holder
Table Cover
Window Valance

Let your imagination be your guide!

Bibliography

There are many books are available on beadwork in general and peyote stitch in particular. This list contains only those which I found useful for designing patterns with diagonal and vertical lines -- the strongest lines created in peyote stitch.

Beveridge, June. *Authentic Algerian Carpet Designs and Motifs.* New York: Dover Publications, Inc., 1978.

Christie, Archibald H. *Traditional Methods of Pattern Designing.* Oxford, England: The Clarendon Press, 1910. (Reprinted by Dover Publications, Co.)

Davis, Mary Kay and Helen Giammattei. *Needlepoint from America's Great Quilt Designs.* New York: Workman Publishing Co., 1974.

Hendler, Muncie. *Infinite Allover Patterns.* New York: Dover Publications, Inc. 1985.

Lantz, Sherlee. *Trianglepoint: From Persian Pavilions to Op Art With One Stitch.* New York: The Viking Press, A Studio Book, 1976.

LaPlantz, Shereen. *The Mad Weave Book.* Bayside, CA: Press de La Plantz, 1984.

Nephew, Sara. *Equilateral Triangle Patchwork.* New York: Dover Publications, 1986.

Pasquini-Masopust, Katie. *Isometric Perspective: From Baby Blocks to Dimensional Design in Quilts.* Lafayette, California: C&T Publishing, 1992.

Perrone, Lisbeth. *The New World of Needlepoint: 101 Exciting Designs in Bargello, Quickpoint, Grospoint and Other Repeat Patterns.* New York: Random House, 1972.

Revault, Jacques. *Designs and Patterns from North African Carpets and Textiles.* New York: Dover Publications, Inc., 1973.

Snook, Barbara. *The Craft of Florentine Embroidery.* New York: Charles Scribner's Sons, 1971.

<u>Beginning Row (Rows 1 & 2)</u>
1M, 7L, 2D

Row 3> 2D, 2L, 1M

Row 4< 2M, 1L, 2D

Row 5> 3D, 2M

Row 6< 3M, 2D

Row 7> 3D, 2M

Row 8< 3M, 2D

Row 9> 3D, 2M

Row 10< 3M, 2D

Row 11> 1L, 2D, 2M

Row 12< 1L, 2M, 1D, 1L

Row 13> 2L, 1D, 1M, 1L

Row 14< 2L, 1M, 2L

Row 15> 5L

Row 16< 2L, 1D, 2L

Row 17> 2L, 1M, 1D, 1L

Row 18< 1L, 2D, 1M, 1L

Row 19> 1L, 2M, 2D

Row 20< 3D, 2M

Row 21> 3M, 2D

Row 22< 3D, 2M

Row 23> 3M, 2D

Row 24< 3D, 2M

Row 25> 3M, 2D

Row 26< 2D, 1L, 2M

Row 27> 2M, 2L, 1D

Row 28< 1D, 3L, 1M

Row 29> 1M, 4L

Row 30< 5L

If you wish to continue with
further repeats of the pattern,
do Rows 1 & 2 below, then
continue with Row 3 above.

Row 1> 1D, 4L

Row 2< 1M, 3L, 1D

Pattern No. 1
Tumbling Blocks

Multiple - 10
Repeat - 30 rows

Colors
L = Light
M = Medium
D = Dark

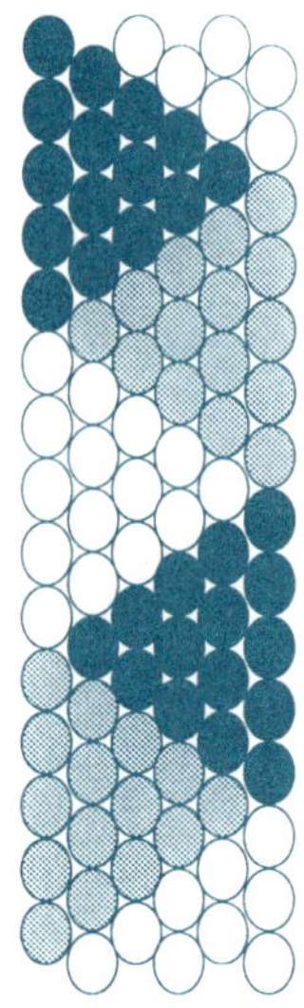

Pattern No. 2
Shadow Triangles

Multiple - 6
Repeat - 30 rows

Colors
L = Light
M = Medium
D = Dark

Beginning Row (Rows 1 & 2)
4L, 2D

Row 3> 2D, 1L

Row 4< 1L, 2D

Row 5> 3D

Row 6< 1M, 2D

Row 7> 2D, 1M

Row 8< 2M, 1D

Row 9> 1D, 2M

Row 10< 3M

Row 11> 1L, 2M

Row 12< 2M, 1L

Row 13>2L, 1M

Row 14< 1M, 2L

Row 15> 3L

Row 16< 1D, 2L

Row 17> 2L, 1D

Row 18< 2D, 1L

Row 19> 1L, 2D

Row 20< 3D

Row 21> 1M, 2D

Row 22< 2D, 1M

Row 23> 2M, 1D

Row 24< 1D, 2M

Row 25> 3M

Row 26< 1L, 2M

Row 27> 2M, 1L

Row 28< 2L, 1M

Row 29> 1M, 2L

Row 30< 3L

If you wish to continue with further repeats of the pattern, do Rows 1 & 2 below, then continue with Row 3 above.

Row 1> 1D, 2L

Row 2< 2L, 1D

<u>Beginning Row (Rows 1 & 2)</u>
3M, 1L, 3D, 5M

Row 3> 2M, 3D, 1M

Row 4< 1M, 4D, 1M

Row 5> 1M, 2D, 1M, 2D

Row 6< 2D, 2M, 2D

Row 7> 2D, 3M, 1D

Row 8< 1D, 4M, 1D

Row 9> 1D, 1L, 4M

Row 10< 4M, 2L

Row 11> 3L, 3M

Row 12< 1L, 2M, 3L

Row 13> 1L, 1M, 2L, 1M, 1L

Row 14< 4L, 2M

Row 15> 3M, 3L

Row 16< 1M, 2L, 3M

If you wish to continue with
further repeats of the pattern,
do Rows 1 & 2 below, then
continue with Row 3 above.

Row 1> 3M, 1D, 1L, 1M

Row 2< 2M, 2D, 2M

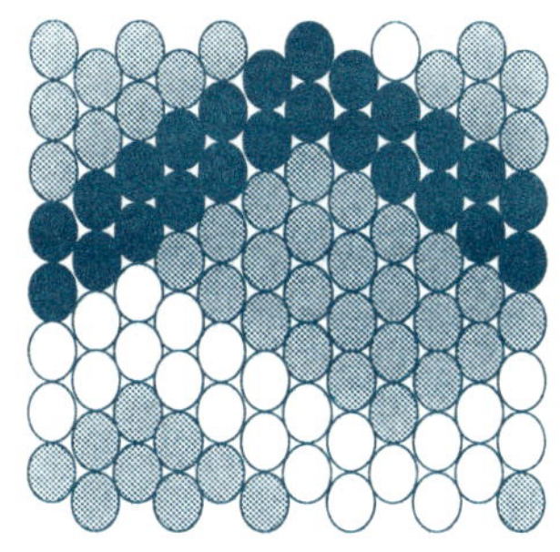

Pattern No. 3
Sine Waves

Multiple: 12
Repeat: 16 rows

Colors
L = Light
M = Medium
D = Dark

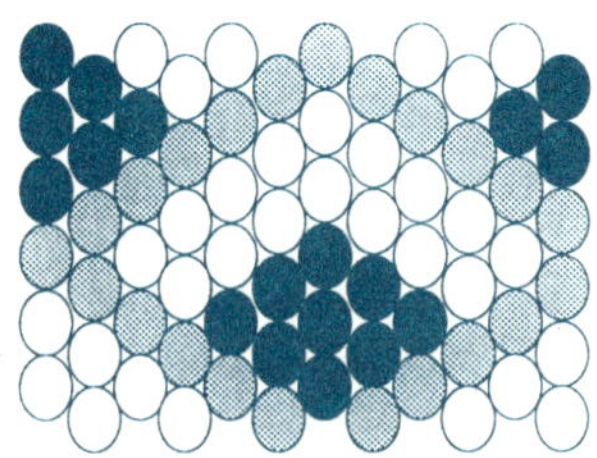

Pattern No. 4
Shadow Boxes

Multiple - 12
Repeat - 12 rows

Colors
L = Light
M = Medium
D = Dark

<u>Beginning Row (Rows 1 & 2)</u>
1D, 3L, 3M, 3L, 2D

Row 3> 2D, 1M, 1L,1M,1D

Row 4< 1D,1M, 2L,1M, 1D

Row 5> 1D,1M,3L,1M,

Row 6< 1M, 4L, 1M

Row 7> 1M, 2L, 1D, 2L

Row 8< 1M, 1L, 2D, 1L, 1M

Row 9> 1L, 1M, 3D, 1M

Row 10< 1L, 1M, 2D, 1M, 1L

Row 11> 2L, 1M, 1D, 1M, 1L

Row 12< 2L, 2M, 2L

If you wish to continue with
further repeats of the pattern,
do Rows 1 & 2 below, then
continue with Row 3 above.

Row 1> 1D, 2L, 1M, 2L

Row 2< 1D, 1L, 2M, 1L, 1D,

<u>Beginning Row (Rows 1 & 2)</u>
1D, 3L, 2D, 1L, 2M, 1D, 2M, 1L, 1D

Row 3> 1D, 1L, 1M, 1L, 3D

Row 4< 1M, 1D, 1M, 1D, 2L, 1D

Row 5> 1L, 1D, 1L, 1D, 1L, 2M

Row 6< 1L, 1M, 1L, 4D

Row 7> 1D, 1M, 1D, 1M, 1D, 2L

Row 8< 1D, 1L, 1D, 1L, 2M, 1L

Row 9> 1D, 1L, 1M, 1L, 3D

Row 10< 1M, 1D, 1M, 1D, 2L, 1D

Row 11> 1L, 1D, 1L, 1D, 1L, 2M

Row 12< 1L, 1M, 1L, 4D

If you wish to continue with further repeats of the
pattern, do Rows 1 & 2 below, then continue with
Row 3 above.

Row 1> 1D, 1M, 1D, 1M, 1D, 2L

Row 2< 1D, 1L, 1D, 1L, 2M, 1L

Pattern No. 5
Layers

Multiple - 14
Repeat - 12 rows

Colors
L= Light
M= Medium
D = Dark

Pattern No. 6
Shoowa

Multiple - 22
Repeat - 26 rows

Colors
L= Light
M= Medium
D = Dark

<u>Beginning Row (Rows 1 & 2)</u>
(2D, 2L) x 2, 2D, 1L, (2D, 2L) x 2, 2D, 1L

Row 3> (1D, 1L) x 3, (1L, 1D) x 2, 1L

Row 4< (1L, 1D) x 2, 1L, 1M, (1L, 1D) x 2, 1L

Row 5> (1L, 1D) x 2, 1L, 1M, 2L, 1D, 1L, 1D

Row 6< (1D, 1L) x 2, (1M, 1L) x 2, 1D, 1L, 1D

Row 7> (1D, 1L) x 2, 1M, 1L, 2M, 1L, 1D, 1L

Row 8< 1L, 1D, (1L, 1M,) x 3, 1L, 1D, 1L

Row 9> 1L, 1D, (1L, 1M) x 2, 2L, 1M, 1L, 1D

Row 10< 1D, (1L, 1M) x 4, 1L, 1D

Row 11> 1D, (1L, 1M) x 2, 1L, 2M, 1L, 1M, 1L

Row 12< (1L, 1M) x 5, 1L

Row 13> (1L, 1M) x 3, 2L, 1M, 1L, 1M

Row 14< (1M, 1L) x 5, 1M

Row 15> (1L, 1M) x 2, 1L, 2M, (1L, 1M) x 2

Row 16< (1L, 1M) x 5, 1L

Row 17> 1D, 1L, 1M, 1L, 1M, 2L, (1M, 1L) x 2

Row 18< 1D, (1L, 1M) x 4, 2L

Row 19> 1L, 1D, 1L, 1M, 1L, 2M, 1L, 1M, 1L, 1D

Row 20< 1L, 1D, (1L, 1M) x 3, 1L, 2D

Row 21> (1D, 1L) x 2, 1M, 2L, 1M, 1L, 1D, 1L

Row 22< (1D, 1L) x 2, (1M, 1L) x 2, 1D, 2L

Row 23> (1L, 1D) x 2, 1L, 2M, (1L, 1D) x 2

Row 24< (1L, 1D) x 2, 1L, 1M, 1L, 1D, 1L, 2D

Row 25> (1D, 1L) x 3, (1L, 1D) x 2, 1L

Row 26< (1D, 1L) x 5, 1L

If you wish to continue with further repeats of the pattern, do Rows 1 & 2 below, then continue with Row 3 above.

Row 1> (1L, 1D) x 3, (1D, 1L) x 2, 1D

Row 2< (1D, 1L) x 5, 1D

<u>Beginning Row (Rows 1 & 2)</u>
1D, 2ML, 2L, 2M, 2L, 1ML, 3D, 2ML, 2L, 2M,
2L, 1ML, 2D

Row 3> 1ML, 1D, 1M, 1L, 1ML, 1D, 1ML, 1D,
1M, 1L, 1ML, 1D

Row 4< 1L, 1D, 1ML, 1L, 1D, 1ML, 1L, 1D,
1ML, 1L, 1D, 1ML

Row 5> 1L, 1ML, 1D, 1ML, 1D, 1M, 1L, 1ML,
1D, 1ML, 1D, 1M

Row 6< 1M, 1L, 2D, 1ML, 1L, 1M, 1L, 2D.
1ML, 1L

Row 7> 1M, 1L, 1ML, 1D, 1ML, 1L, 1M, 1L,
1ML, 1D, 1ML, 1L

Row 8< 1L, 1ML, 2D, 1L, 1M, 1L, 1ML, 2D,
1L, 1M

Row 9> 1L, 1M, 1D, 1ML, 1D, 1ML, 1L, 1M,
1D, 1ML, 1D, 1ML

Row 10< 1ML, 1D, 1L, 1ML, 1D, 1L, 1ML, 1D,
1L, 1ML, 1D, 1L

Row 11> 1ML, 1D, 1ML, 1L, 1M, 1D, 1ML,
1D, 1ML, 1L, 1M, 1D

Row 12< 1D, 1L, 1M, 1L, 1ML, 2D, 1L, 1M,
1L, 1ML, 1D

If you wish to continue with further repeats of the
pattern, do Rows 1 & 2 below, then continue with
Row 3 above.

Row 1> 1D, 1ML, 1L, 1M, 1L, 1ML, 1D, 1ML,
1L, 1M, 1L, 1ML

Row 2< 1D, 1ML, 1L, 1M, 1L, 2D, 1ML, 1L,
1M, 1L, 1D

Pattern No. 7
Basket Weave

Multiple - 24
Repeat - 12 rows

Colors
L = Light
ML= Medium Light
B = Medium
D = Dark

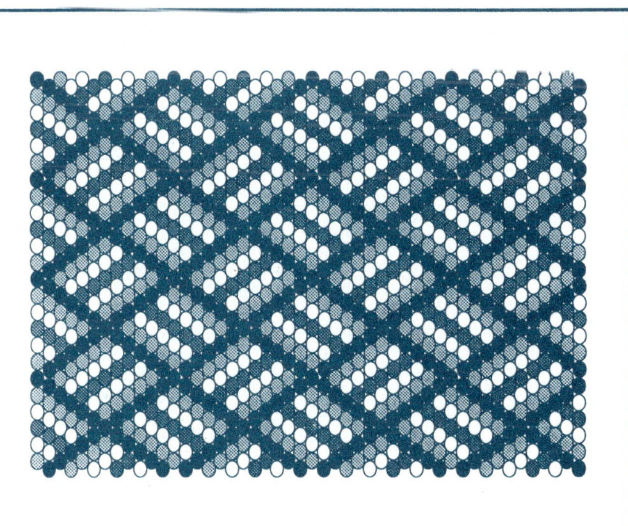

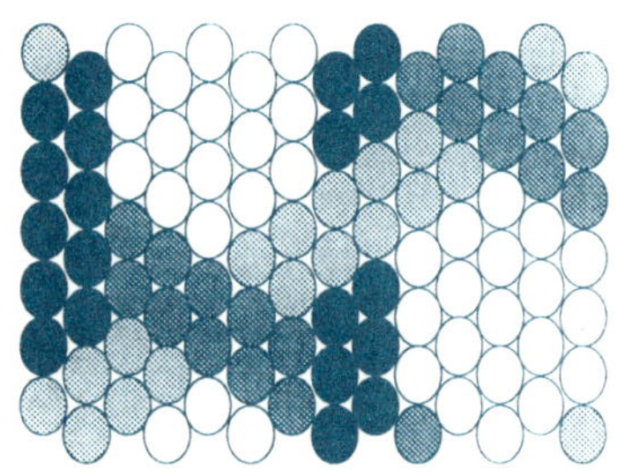

Pattern No. 8
Triaxial Weave

Multiple - 14
Repeat - 14 rows

Colors
L = Light
ML = Medium Light
M = Medium
D = Dark

2ML, 3M, 2D, 5L, 1D, 1ML

Row 3> 1D, 3L, 1D, 2M

Row 4< 2M, 1ML, 1D, 2L, 1D

Row 5> 1D, 3L, 2ML, 1M

Row 6< 1M, 1L, 2ML, 2L, 1D

Row 7> 1D, 1M, 1L, 2ML, 2L

Row 8> 3L, 2ML, 1M, 1D

Row 9> 1D, 2M, 1ML, 1D, 2L

Row 10< 3L, 1D, 2M, 1D

Row 11> 1D, 1ML, 2M, 1D, 2L

Row 12< 3L, 1D, 1M, 2ML,

Row 13> 2ML, 1L, 1M, 1D, 2L

Row 14< 1ML, 1L, 1M, 1D, 2L, 1ML

If you wish to continue with further repeats of the pattern, do Rows 1 & 2 below, then continue with Row 3 above.

Row 1> 1ML, 3L, 1D, 1M, 1ML

Row 2< 1ML, 2M, 1D, 2L, 1D

<u>Beginning Row (Rows 1 & 2)</u>
3D, 1L, 3D, 1L

Row 3> 1M, 3D

Row 4< 1L, 2D, 1L

Row 5> 1M, 3D

Row 6< 1M, 2D, 1M

Row 7> 1M, 1L, 1D, 1L

Row 8< 1M, 2D, 1M

Row 9> 2M, 1D, 1M

Row 10<1M, 2L, 1M

Row 11> 2M, 1D, 1M

Row 12< 4M

Row 13> 1L, 1M, 1L, 1M

Row 14< 4M

Row 15> 1D, 3M

Row 16< 1L, 2M, 1L

Row 17>1D, 3M

Row 18< 1D, 2M, 1D

Row 19> 1D, 1L, 1M, 1L

Row 20< 1D, 2M, 1D

Row 21> 2D, 1M, 1D

Row 22< 1D, 2L, 1D

Row 23> 2D, 1M, 1D

Row 24< 4D

If you wish to continue with further repeats of the pattern, do Rows 1 & 2 below, then continue with Row 3 above.

Row 1> 1L, 1D, 1L, 1D

Row 2< 4D

Pattern No. 9
Jaws

Multiple - 8
Repeat - 24 rows

Colors
L = Light
M = Medium
D = Dark

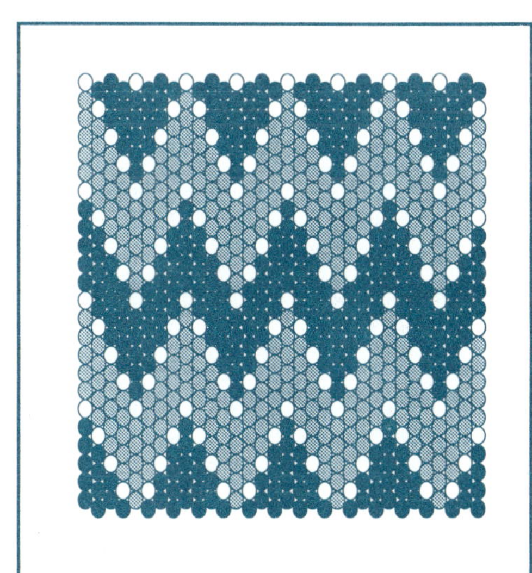

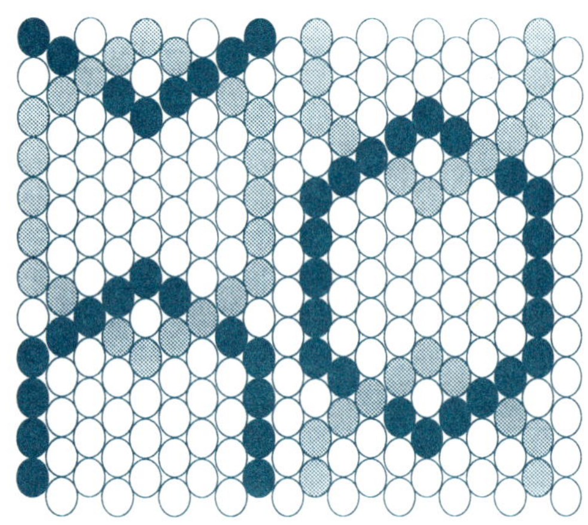

Pattern No. 10
Chains

Multiple - 20
Repeat - 24 rows

Colors
L = Light
M = Medium
D = Dark

<u>Beginning Row (Rows 1 & 2)</u>
1L, 1M, 7L, 1M, 1L, 2D, 1L, 3M, 1L, 2D

Row 3> 1L, 1M, 1L, 1D, 1L, 1M, 3L, 1M

Row 4< 6L, 1M, 2D, 1M

Row 5> 1M, 1L, 1D, 1L, 2M, 1L, 1D, 1L, 1M

Row 6< 1L, 1M, 2D, 1M, 5L

Row 7> 1M, 3L, 1M, 1L, 1D, 1L, 1M, 1L

Row 8< 1L, 1D, 2M, 1D, 5L

Row 9> 1M, 3L, 1M, 1D, 1L, 1M, 1L, 1D

Row 10< 10L

Row 11> 1M, 3L, 1M, 1D, 3L, 1D

Row 12< 10L

Row 13> 1M, 1L, 1D, 1L, 1M, 1D, 3L, 1D

Row 14< 6L, 1M, 2D, 1M

Row 15> 1L, 1D, 1L, 1M, 1L, 1D, 3L, 1D

Row 16< 6L, 1D, 2M, 1D

Row 17> 1D, 1L, 1M, 1L, 2D, 1L, 1M, 1L, 1D

Row 18< 1L, 1D, 2M, 1D, 5L

Row 19> 1D, 3L, 1D, 1L, 1M, 1L, 1D, 1L

Row 20< 1L, 1M, 2D, 1M, 5L

Row 21> 1D, 3L, 1D, 1M, 1L, 1D, 1L, 1M

Row 22< 10L

Row 23> 1D, 3L, 1D, 1M, 3L, 1M

Row 24< 10L

If you wish to continue with further repeats of the pattern, do Rows 1 & 2 below, then continue with Row 3 above.

Row 1> 1D, 1L, 1M, 1L, 1D, 1M, 3L, 1M

Row 2< 6L, 1D, 2M, 1D

<u>Beginning Row (Rows 1 & 2)</u>
2M, 2ML, 2L, 2D, 1L, 1ML, 1L, 2D, 2L, 2ML, 1M

Row 3> 1ML, 1L, 1D, 1L, 1ML, 1L, 1D, 1L, 1ML

Row 4< 1ML, 1L, 1D, 1L, 2ML, 1L, 1D, 1L

Row 5> 1L, 1D, 1L, 1ML, 1M, 1ML, 1L, 1D, 1L

Row 6< 1ML, 1D, 1L, 1ML, 2M, 1ML, 1L, 1D

Row 7> 2L, 1ML, 1M, 1D, 1M, 1ML, 2L

Row 8< 1ML, 1D, 1ML, 1M, 2D, 1M, 1ML, 1D

Row 9> 2L, 1M, 1D, 1M, 1D, 1M, 2L

Row 10< (1ML, 1D X 2), 2M, 1D, 1ML, 1D

Row 11> 2L, 2M, 1ML, 2M, 2L

Row 12< 1L, 1D, 1ML, 1D, 2ML, 1D, 1ML, 1D

Row 13> 1D, 1L, 2M, 1L, 2M, 1L, 1D

Row 14< 1D, 1L, 1ML, 1D, 2ML, 1D, 1ML, 1L

Row 15> 1L, 1ML, 2M, 1L, 2M, 1ML, 1L

Row 16< 1L, 1ML, 1M, 1D, 2ML, 1D, 1M, 1ML

Row 17> 1ML, 1M, 1D, 1M, 1L, 1M, 1D, 1M, 1ML

Row 18< 1L, 1M, 1D, 1M, 2ML, 1M, 1D, 1M

Row 19> 1ML, 1D, 1M, 1ML, 1L, 1ML, 1M, 1D, 1ML

Row 20< 1L, 2M, 1ML, 2L, 1ML, 2M

Row 21> 1ML, 1D, 1ML, 1L, 1D, 1L, 1ML, 1D, 1ML

Row 22< 1L, 2M, 1L, 2D, 1L, 2M

Row 23> 1ML, 1D, 1ML, 1D, 1L, 1D, 1ML, 1D, 1ML

Row 24< 1ML, 2M, 4L, 2M

Row 25> 1M, 1D, 1ML, 1D, 1ML, 1D, 1ML, 1D, 1M

Row 26< 1M, 1D, 1M, 4L, 1M, 1D

Row 27> 1D, 1M, 1ML, 1D, 1ML, 1D, 1ML, 1M, 1D

Row 28< 1D, 1M, 1ML, 4L, 1ML, 1M

If you wish to continue with further repeats of the pattern,
do Rows 1 & 2 below, then continue with Row 3 above.

Row 1> 1M, 1ML, 1L, 1D, 1ML, 1D, 1L, 1ML, 1M

Row 2< 1M, 1ML, 1L, 1D, 2L, 1D, 1L, 1ML

Pattern No. 11
Prayer Rug

Multiple - 18
Repeat -   28 rows

Colors
L = Light
ML = Medium Light
M = Medium
D = Dark

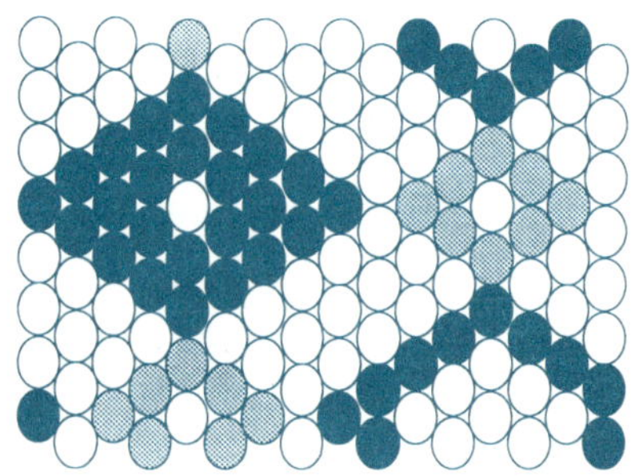

Pattern No. 12
Beaded Curtain

Multiple - 16
Repeat - 16 rows

Colors
L = Light
M = Medium
D = Dark

<u>Beginning Row (Rows 1 & 2)</u>
1L, 2D, 1L, 2D, 5L, 1M, 4L

Row 3> 2L, 1D, 3L, 1D, 1L

Row 4< 5L, 2D, 1L

Row 5> 1L, 3D, 2L, 1M, 1L

Row 6< 1L, 2M, 1L, 4D

Row 7> 2D, 1L, 2D, 1M, 1L, 1M

Row 8< 1L, 2M, 1L, 4D

Row 9> 1L, 3D, 2L, 1M, 1L

Row 10< 5L, 2D, 1L

Row 11> 2L, 1D, 3L, 1D, 1L

Row 12< 1L, 2D, 5L

Row 13> 2L, 1M, 2L, 1D, 1L, 1D

Row 14< 1D, 2L, 1D, 1L, 2M, 1L

Row 15>1D, 1M, 1L, 1M, 1D, 3L

Row 16< 1D, 2L, 1D, 1L, 2M, 1L

If you wish to continue with further repeats of the pattern, do Rows 1 & 2 below, then continue with Row 3 above.

Row 1> 2L, 1M, 2L, 1D, 1L, 1D

Row 2< 1L, 2D, 5L

Beginning Row (Rows 1 & 2)
6L, 3D, 11L

Row 3> 5L, 1D, 1L, 1D, 2L

Row 4< 3L, 2D, 5L

Row 5> 4L, 1M, 1L, 1D, 1L, 1M, 1L

Row 6< 1L, 2M, 2D, 2M, 3L

Row 7> 3L, 1M, 1L, 1M, 1L, 1D, 1L, 1M

Row 8< 1M, 1L, 1D, 2M, 1D, 1L, 1M, 2L

Row 9> 1M, 1L, 1M, 1L, 1D, 1L, 1M, 1L, 1D, 1L

Row 10< 1M, 1D, 4L, 1D, 1M, 2L

Row 11> 1L, 1D, 1L, 1D, 5L, 1M

Row 12< 1D, 1M, 4L, 1M, 3D

Row 13> 1D, 1L, 1D, 1L, 1M, 3L, 1M, 1L

Row 14< 1D, 1M, 4L, 1M, 3D

Row 15> 1L, 1D, 1L, 1M, 5L, 1D

Row 16< 1M, 1D, 4L, 1D, 1M, 2L

Row 17> 1M, 1L, 1M, 1L, 1D, 1L, 1M, 1L, 1D, 1L

Row 18< 1M, 1L, 1D, 2M, 1D, 1L, 1M, 2L

Row 19> 3L, 1M, 1L, 1D, 1L, 1M, 1L, 1M

Row 20< 1L, 2M, 2D, 2M, 3L

If you wish to continue with further repeats of the
pattern, do Rows 1 & 2 below, then continue with Row
3 above.

Row 1> 6L, 1D, 3L

Row 2< 3L, 2D, 5L

Pattern No. 13
Coptic Knot

Multiple - 20
Repeat - 20 rows

Colors
L = Light
M = Medium
D = Dark

Pattern No. 14
Braids

Multiple - 8
Repeat - 24 rows

Colors
L = Light
M = Medium
D = Dark

<u>Beginning Row (Rows 1 & 2)</u>
5L, 1D, 2M

Row 3> 2M, 1L, 1D

Row 4< 1L, 1D, 2M

Row 5> 1L, 1M, 2D

Row 6< 1L, 2D, 1L

Row 7> 2L, 1D, 1M

Row 8< 1L, 1M, 2L

Row 9> 1D, 1L, 2M

Row 10< 1L, 2M, 1D

Row 11> 2D, 1M, 1L

Row 12< 2L, 2D

Row 13> 1M, 1D, 2L

Row 14< 3L, 1M

Row 15> 2M, 1L, 1D

Row 16< 1L, 1D, 2M

Row 17> 1L, 1M, 2D

Row 18< 1L, 2D, 1L

Row 19> 2L, 1D, 1M

Row 20< 1L, 1M, 2L

Row 21> 1D, 1L, 2M

Row 22< 1L, 2M, 1D

Row 23> 2D, 1M, 1L

Row 24< 2L, 2D

If you wish to continue with further repeats of the pattern, do Rows 1 & 2 below, then continue with Row 3 above.

Row 1> 1M, 1D, 2L

Row 2< 3L, 1M

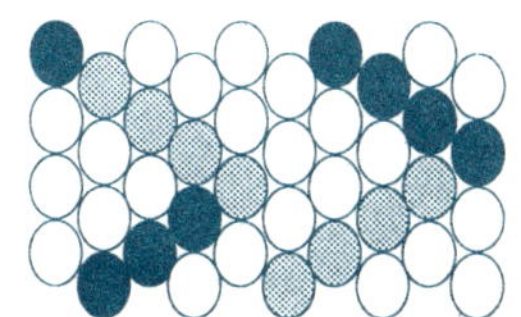

<u>Beginning Row (Rows 1 & 2)</u>
2L, 2D, 4L, 1M, 1D

Row 3> 1L, 1M, 2L, 1D

Row 4< 1D, 2L, 1M, 1L

Row 5> 2L, 1M, 1L, 1M

Row 6< 1L, 1M, 1L, 1D, 1L

Row 7> 1L, 1D, 1L, 1M, 1L

Row 8< 2L, 1M, 1L, 1D

If you wish to continue with
further repeats of the pattern, do
Rows 1 & 2 below, then continue with Row 3 above.

Row 1> 1D, 2L, 1D, 1L

Row 2< 1L, 1D, 2L, 1M

Pattern No. 15
Worm Convention

Multiple - 10
Repeat - 8 rows

Colors
L = Light
M = Medium
D = Dark

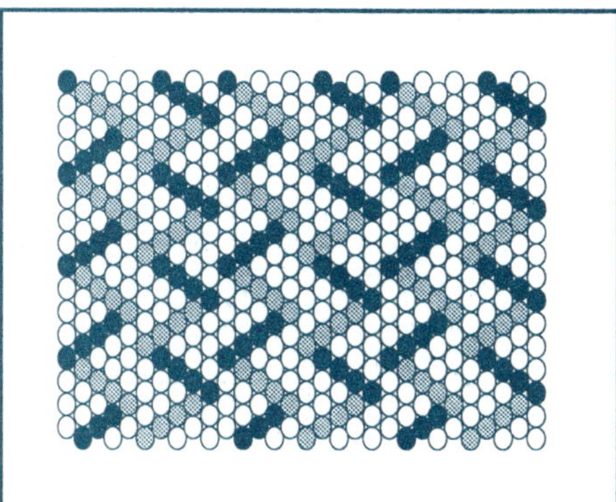

Pattern No. 16
God's Eye

Multiple - 34
Repeat - 38 rows

Colors
L = Light
M = Medium
D = Dark

2M, 2L, 2M, 4L, 2M, 1D, 2L, 5M, 2L, 1D, 2M, 4L, 2M, 2L, 1M

Row 3> 1L, 1M, 2L, 1M, 1L, 1D, 1L, 1M, 1L, 1D, 1L, 1M, 2L, 1M, 1L

Row 4< 1L, 1M, 2L, 1M, 2L, 1D, 2L, 1D, 2L, 1M, 2L, 1M

Row 5> 1M, 2L, 1M, (1L, 1D) x 4, 1L, 1M, 2L, 1M

Row 6< (1M, 2L)x2, 1D, 1L, 2D, 1L, 1D, 2L, 1M, 2L

Row 7> 2L, 1M, (1L, 1D) x 5, 1L, 1M, 2L

Row 8< 2L, 1M, 2L, 1D, 1L, 4D, 1L, 1D, 2L, 1M, 1L

Row 9> 1L, 1M, (1L, 1D) x 6, 1L, 1M, 1L

Row 10< 1L, 1M, 2L, 1D, 1L, 2D, 2L, 2D, 1L, 1D, 2L, 1M

Row 11> 1M, (1L, 1D) x 7, 1L, 1M

Row 12< 1M, 2L, 1D, 1L, (2D, 1L)x3,1D, 2L

Row 13> (1L, 1D) x 3, 1L, 3D, (1L, 1D) x 3, 1L

Row 14< (1D, 1L) x 2, 2D, 1L, 4D, 1L, 2D, 1L, 1D, 1L

Row 15> (1D, 1L) x 3, 2D, 1L, 2D, (1L, 1D) x 3

Row 16< 1L, 1D, (1L, 2D) x 2, 2L, (2D, 1L) x 2,1D

Row 17> (1L, 1D)x2, 1L, 2D, 1L, 1M, 1L, 2D, (1L, 1D) x 2, 1L

Row 18< 1M, (1L, 2D) x 2,1L, 2M, (1L, 2D) x 2, 1L

Pattern No. 16, Cont'd.

Row 19> 1M, 1L, 1D, 1L, 2D, 1L, 3M, 1L, 2D, 1L, 1D, 1L, 1M

Row 20< 2M, 1D, 1L, 2D, 1L, 4M, 1L, 2D, 1L, 1D, 1M

Row 21> 1M, 1L, 1D, 1L, 2D, 1L, 3M, 1L, 2D, 1L, 1D, 1L, 1M

Row 22< 1M, (1L, 2D) x 2, 1L, 2M, 1L, (2D, 1L) x 2

Row 23> (1L, 1D) x 2, 1L, 2D, 1L, 1M, 1L, 2D, (1L, 1D) x 2, 1L

Row 24< 1L, 1D, 1L, 2D, 1L, 2D, 2L, 2D, 1L, 2D, 1L, 1D

Row 25> (1D, 1L) x 3, 2D, 1L, 2D, (1L, 1D) x 3

Row 26< (1D, 1L) x 2, 2D, 1L, 4D, 1L, 2D, 1L, 1D, 1L

Row 27> (1L, 1D) x 3, 1L, 3D, (1L, 1D) x 3, 1L

Row 28< 1M, 2L, 1D, (1L, 2D) x 3, 1L, 1D, 2L

Row 29> 1M, (1L, 1D) x 7, 1L, 1M

Row 30< 1L, 1M, 2L, 1D, 1L, 2D, 2L, 2D, 1L, 1D, 2L, 1M

Row 31> 1L, 1M, (1L, 1D) x 6, 1L, 1M, 1L

Row 32< 2L, 1M, 2L, 1D, 1L, 4D, 1L, 1D, 2L, 1M, 1L

Row 33> 2L, 1M, (1L, 1D) x 5, 1L, 1M, 2L

Row 34< (1M, 2L) x 2, 1D, 1L, 2D, 1L, 1D, 2L, 1M, 2L

Row 35> 1M, 2L, 1M, (1L, 1D) x 4, 1L, 1M, 2L, 1M

Row 36< 1L, 1M, 2L, 1M, 2L, 1D, 2L, 1D, 2L, 1M, 2L, 1M

Row 37> 1L, 1M, 2L, 1M, 1L, 1D, 1L, 1M, 1L, 1D, 1L, 1M, 2L, 1M, 1L

Row 38< 1M, 1L, 1M, 2L, 1M, 1D, 1L, 2M, 1L, 1D, 1M, 2L, 1M, 1L

If you wish to continue with further repeats of the pattern, do Rows 1 & 2 below, then continue with Row 3 above.

Row 1> 1M, 1L, 1M, 2L, 1M, 1L, 3M, 1L, 1M, 2L, 1M, 1L, 1M

Row 2< 1M, 1L, 1M, 2L, 1L, 1D, 1L, 2M, 1L, 1D, 1M, 2L, 1M, 1L

Pattern No. 17
Birds and Clouds

Multiple - 28
Repeat - 28 rows

Colors
L = Light
M = Medium
D = Dark

<u>Beginning Row (Rows 1 & 2)</u>
1D, 1L, 3D, 1L, 2D, 3L, 2M, 2L,
2M, 2L, 1M, 2L, 2M, 3L, 1D

Row 3> 1L, 1D, (1L, 1M) x 3, (1L,
1D) x 3

Row 4< 1D, 2L, 3D, 1L, 1M, 1L,
1M, 2L, 2D

Row 5> (1D, 1L) x 2, (1M, 1L) x 2,
(1D, 1L) x 3

Row 6< 1D, 2L, 3D, 2L, (1M, 1L)
x 2, 2D

Row 7> 1L, 1D, (1L, 1M) x 3, (1L,
1D) x 3

Row 8< 4D, (2L, 1M) x 2, 1L, 1M,
2L

Row 9> 1D, 1L, (1M, 1L) x 4, (1D,
1L) x 2

Row 10< 1L, 2D, 2L, 1M, 1L, 1M,
2L, (1M, 1L) x 2

Row 11> (1L, 1M) x 2, 1L, 1D,
(1L, 1M) x 2, (1L, 1D) x 2

Row 12< 1L, 2D, (1L, 1M) x 2, 1L,
1D, 2L, 1M, 1L, 1M

Row 13> (1M, 1L) x 2,
(1D, 1L) x 2, (1M, 1L) x 2, 1D, 1L

Row 14< 1M, 2L, 1M, 1L, 1M, 2L,
2D, 2L, 1M, 1L

Row 15> 1L, 1M, (1L, 1D) x 2, 3L,
(1M, 1L) x 2, 1M

Row 16< 2L, (1M, 1L) x 2, 1D, 2L,
2D, 2L, 1M

Row 17> 1M, 1L, 1D, 1L, 1D, 2L,
2D, (1L, 1M) x 2, 1L

Row 18< (1L, 1M) x 2, (1L, 1D) x 2, 1L, 4D, 1L

Row 19> (1L, 1D) x 3, 1L, 3D, (1L, 1M) x 2

Row 20< 1M, 1L, 1M, 3L, 1D, 1L, 4D, 2L

Row 21> 1M, (1L, 1D) x 4, (1L, 1M) x 2, 1L

Row 22< 1L, 1M, 2L, 1M, 1L, 4D, 1L, 1D, 1L, 1M

Row 23> 1L, 1M, 3L, (1D, 1L) x 2, (1M, 1L) x 2, 1M

Row 24< 1M, 2L, (1M, 1L) x 2, 3D, 2L, 1M, 1L

Row 25> (1M, 1L) x 2, (1D, 1L) x 2, (1M, 1L) x 2, 1D, 1L

Row 26< 1L, 2D, (1L, 1M) x 2, 2L, 1D, (1L, 1M) x 2

Row 27> (1L, 1M) x 2, 1L, 1D, (1L, 1M) x 2, (1L, 1D) x 2

Row 28< 1L, 2D, 2L, 1M, 1L, 1M, 2L, (1M, 1L) x 2

If you wish to continue with further repeats of the pattern,
do Rows 1 & 2 below, then continue with Row 3 above.

Row 1>1D, (1L, 1M) x 4, (1L, 1D) x 2, 1L

Row 2< 1D, 2L, 1M, 1L, (1M, 2L) x 2

Pattern No. 18
Persian Stars

Multiple - 26
Repeat - 26 rows

Colors
L = Light
M = Medium
D = Dark

1D, 5L, 2M, 1L, 1M, 3L, 1M, 1L, 2M, 5L, 4D

Row 3> 2D, 2L, (1M, 1L X 4), 1L

Row 4< 1D, 1L, 1M, 6L, 1M, 1L, 2D

Row 5> 3D, 1M, 1L, 1D, 1M, 1L, 1M, 1D, 1L, 1M, 1D

Row 6< 2D, 1L, 1D, 4L, 1D, 1L, 3D

Row 7> 3D, 1M, 1L, 1D, 1M, 1L, 1M, 1D, 1L, 1M, 1D

Row 8< 1D, 1L, 1M, 6L, 1M, 1L, 2D

Row 9> 2D, 2L, 1M, (1L, 1M X 3), 2L

Row 10< 1D, 2L, 1M, 4L, 1M, 2L, 2D

Row 11> 2D, 3L, 2M, 1L, 2M, 3L

Row 12< 1D, 3L, 1M, 2L, 1M, 3L, 1D, 1L

Row 13> 2L, 1M, 3L, 1D, 1L, 1D, 3L, 1M

Row 14< 2M, 3L, 2D, 3L, 2M, 1L

Row 15> 3L, 1M, 2L, 3D, 2L, 1M, 1L

Row 16< 1M, 1L, 1M, 2L, 2D, 2L, (1M, 1L X 2)

Row 17> 4L, 1M, 1L, 3D, 1L, 1M, 2L

Row 18< 1M, 1D, 1L, 1M, 4D, 1M, 1L, 1D, 1M, 1L

Row 19> 3L, 1D, 1L, 5D, 1L, 1D, 1L

Row 20< 1M, 1D, 1L, 1M, 4D, 1M, 1L, 1D, 1M, 1L

Pattern No. 18, Con't.

Row 21> 4L, 1M, 1L, 3D, 1L, 1M, 2L

Row 22< 1M, 1L, 1M, 2L, 2D, 2L, (1M, 1L X 2)

Row 23> 3L, 1M, 2L, 3D, 2L, 1M, 1L

Row 24< 2M, 3L, 2D, 3L, 2M, 1L

Row 25> 2L, 1M, 3L, 1D, 1L, 1D, 3L, 1M

Row 26< 1D, 3L, 1M, 2L, 1M, 3L, 1D, 1L

If you wish to continue with further repeats of the pattern,
do Rows 1 & 2 below, then continue with Row 3 above.

Row 1> 2D, 3L, 2M, 1L, 2M, 3L

Row 2< 1D, 2L, 1M, 4L, 1M, 2L, 2D

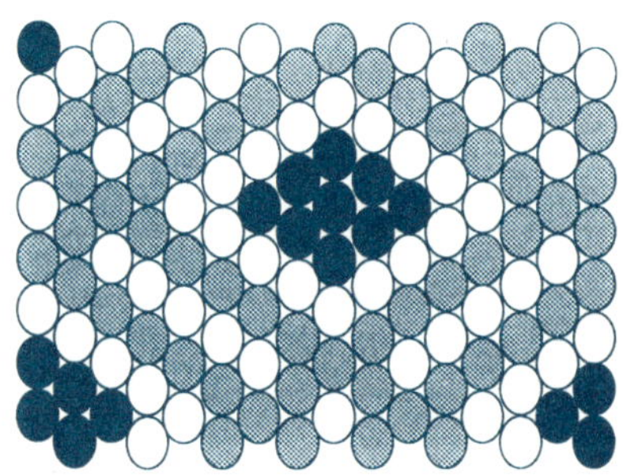

Pattern No. 19
Crossroads

Multiple - 16
Repeat - 16 rows

Colors
L = Light
M = Medium
D = Dark

Beginning Row (Rows 1 & 2)
2L, 2M, 2L, 3M, 2L, 2M, 2L 1D

Row 3> (1L, 1M X 4)

Row 4< 1M, 1L, 1M, 2L, 1M, 1L, 1M

Row 5> (1M, 1L X 2), 1D, 1L, 1M, 1L

Row 6< 2M, 1L, 2D, 1L, 2M

Row 7> 1L, 1M, 1L, 3D, 1L, 1M

Row 8< 2M, 1L, 2D, 1L, 2M

Row 9> (1M, 1L X 2), 1D, 1L, 1M, 1L

Row 10< (1M, 1L X 2), (1L, 1M X 2)

Row 11> (1L, 1M X 4)

Row 12< (1L, 1M X 2), (1M, 1L X 2)

Row 13> 1D, (1L, 1M X 3), 1L

Row 14< 1D, 1L, 4M, 1L, 1D

Row 15> 2D, (1L, 1M X 2), 1L, 1D

Row 16< 1D, 1L, 4M, 1L, 1D

If you wish to continue with further repeats
of the pattern, do Rows 1 & 2 below,
then continue with Row 3 above.

Row 1> 1D, (1L, 1M X 3), 1L

Row 2< (1L, 1M X 2), (1M, 1L X 2)

<u>Beginning Row (Rows 1 & 2)</u>
1D, 1M, 1L, 1M, 2ML, 1L, 1D

Row 3> 1L, 1D, 1M, 1D

Row 4< 1L, 1D, 1L, 1D

Row 5> 1D, 1M, 1D, 1L

Row 6< 1D, 1L, 1ML, 1L

Row 7> 2M, 1ML, 1D

Row 8< 1L, 1ML, 2L

Row 9> 2M, 1L, 1ML

Row 10< 1ML, 1L, 1ML, 1L

Row 11> 2M, 1ML, 1L

Row 12< 1L, 1ML, 2L

Row 13> 2M, 1D, 1M

Row 14< 1ML, 1L, 1D, 1L

Row 15> 1M, 1D, 1L, 1D

Row 16< 1L, 1D, 1L, 1D

Row 17> 1D, 1L, 1D, 1M

Row 18< 1ML, 1L, 1D, 1L

Row 19> 1ML, 1D, 2M

Row 20< 3L, 1ML

Row 21> 1L, 1ML, 2M,

Row 22< 1ML, 1L, 1ML, 1L

Row 23> 1ML, 1L, 2M

Row 24< 3L, 1M

If you wish to continue with further repeats of the
pattern, do Rows 1 & 2 below, then continue with
Row 3 above.

Row 1> 1D, 1ML, 2M

Row 2< 1D, 1L, 1ML, 1L

Pattern No. 20
Mobius Triangle

Multiple - 8
Repeat - 24 rows

Colors
L = Light
ML= Medium Light
B = Medium
D = Dark

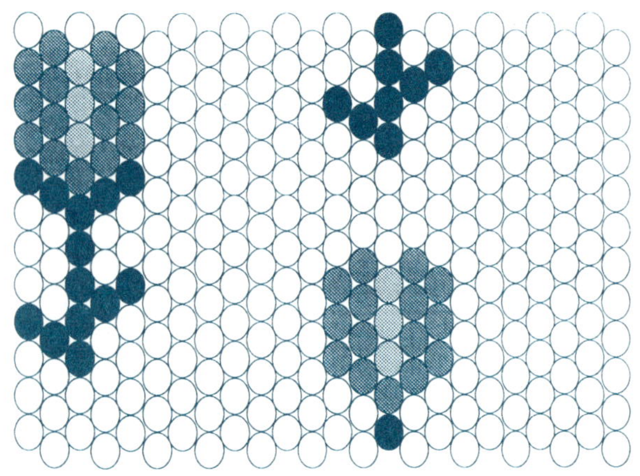

Pattern No. 21
Flower Garden

Multiple - 24
Repeat - 24 rows

Colors
L = Light
ML= Medium Light
M = Medium
D = Dark

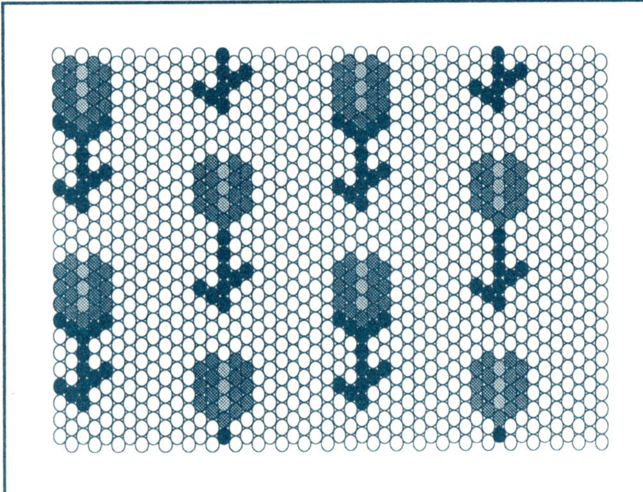

<u>Beginning Row (Rows 1 & 2)</u>
9L, 1D, 10L, 1M, 1L, 1M, 1L

Row 3> 1M, 1ML, 1M, 4L, 2D, 3L

Row 4< 4L, 1D, 5L, 2M

Row 5> 1M, 1ML, 1M, 3L, 2D, 4L

Row 6< 5L, 1D, 4L, 2M

Row 7> 1M, 1ML, 1M, 4L, 1D, 4L

Row 8< 10L, 2M

Row 9> 1D, 1M, 1D, 9L

Row 10< 10L, 2D

Row 11> 1L, 1D, 10L

Row 12< 12L

Row 13> 1L, 1D, 10L

Row 14< 4L, 2M, 6L

Row 15> 1L, 2D, 3L, 1M, 1ML, 1M, 3L

Row 16< 4L, 2M, 4L, 1D, 1L

Row 17> 2D, 4L, 1M, 1ML, 1M, 3L

Row 18< 4L, 2M, 5L, 1D

Row 19> 1L, 1D, 4L, 1M, 1ML, 1M, 3L

Row 20< 4L, 2M, 6L

Row 21> 7L, 1M, 4L

Row 22< 12L

Row 23> 7L, 1D, 4L

Row 24< 12L

If you wish to continue with further repeats of the pattern, do Rows 1 & 2 below, then continue with Row 3 above.

Row 1> 7L, 1D, 4L

Row 2< 10L, 2M

<u>Beginning Row (Rows 1 & 2)</u>
4L, 3M, 5L

Row 3> 2L, 3M, 1L

Row 4< 1L, 3M, 1D, 1L

Row 5> 1L, 1M, 1D, 1M, 1ML, 1M

Row 6< 2M, 1ML, 2D, 1M

Row 7> 2M, 1D, 2ML, 1M

Row 8< 2M, 1ML, 2D, 1M

Row 9> 2M, 1D, 2ML, 1M

Row 10< 1M, 1L, 1ML, 1D, 1L, 1M

Row 11> 1M, 2L, 1ML, 2L

Row 12< 6L

Row 13> 1M, 2L, 1D, 2L

Row 14< 1M, 1L, 1D, 1ML, 1L, 1M

Row 15> 2M, 1ML, 2D, 1M

Row 16< 2M, 1D, 2ML, 1M

Row 15> 2M, 1ML, 2D, 1M

Row 17<2M, 1D, 2ML, 1M

Row 18>1L, 1M, 1ML, 1M, 1D, 1M

Row 19< 1L, 3M, 1ML, 1L

Row 20> 2L, 3M, 1L

Row 21< 2L, 2M, 2L

Row 22> 3L, 1M, 2L

Row 23< 6L

If you wish to continue with further repeats of the pattern, do Rows 1 & 2 below, then continue with Row 3 above.

Row 1> 3L, 1M, 2L

Row 2< 2L, 2M, 2L

Pattern No. 22
Hex Signs

Multiple - 12
Repeat -   24 rows

Colors
L = Light
ML = Medium Light
M = Medium
D = Dark

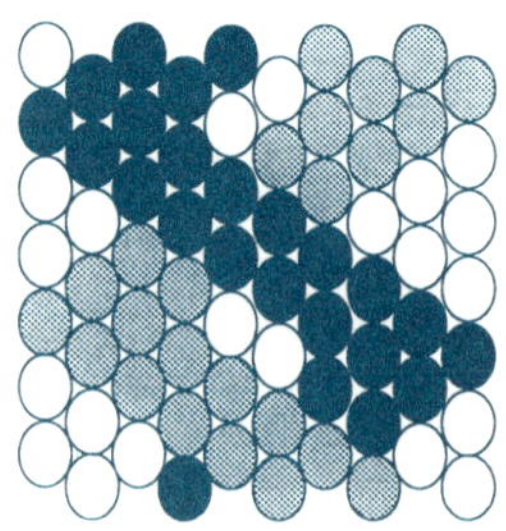

4M, 1L, 4D, 1L

Row 3> 2D, 1L, 2M

Row 4< 1L, 2M, 2D

Row 5> 1L, 2D, 1M, 1L

Row 6< 2L, 2D, 1L

Row 7> 1L, 1M, 2D, 1L

Row 8< 1L, 2D, 2M

Row 9> 2M, 1L, 2D

Row 10< 2D, 1L, 2M

Row 11> 1L, 2M, 2D

Row 12< 1L, 1D, 2M, 1L

Row 13> 2L, 2M, 1L

Row 14< 1L, 2M, 1D, 1L

If you wish to continue with further repeats of the pattern, do Rows 1 & 2 below, then continue with Row 3 above.

Row 1> 1L, 2D, 2M

Row 2< 2M, 1L, 2D

Pattern No. 23
Embrace

Multiple - 10
Repeat - 14 rows

Colors
L = Light
M = Medium
D = Dark

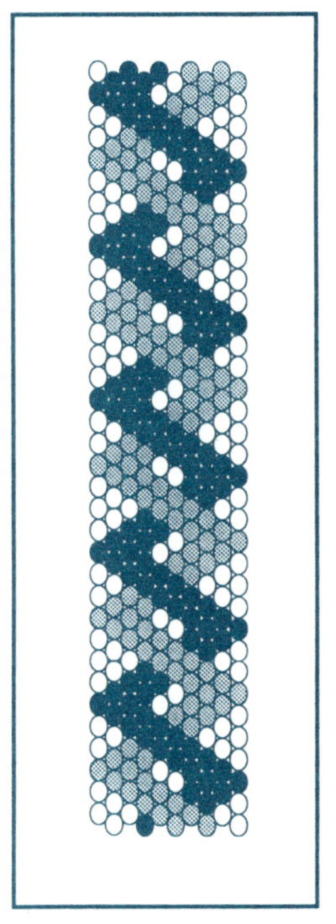

1L, 2M, 2L, 2D, 1L

Row 3> 2D, 2M

Row 4< 1L, 1M, 1L, 1D

Row 5> 1L, 1D, 1L, 1M

Row 6< 4L

If you wish to continue with further repeats of the pattern, do Rows 1 & 2 below, then continue with Row 3 above.

Row 1> 1L, 1D, 1L, 1M

Row 2< 1L, 1M, 1L, 1D

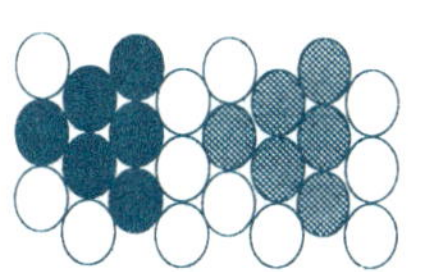

Pattern No. 24
Egyptian Cuff

Multiple - 8
Repeat - 6 rows

Colors
L = Light
B = Medium
D = Dark

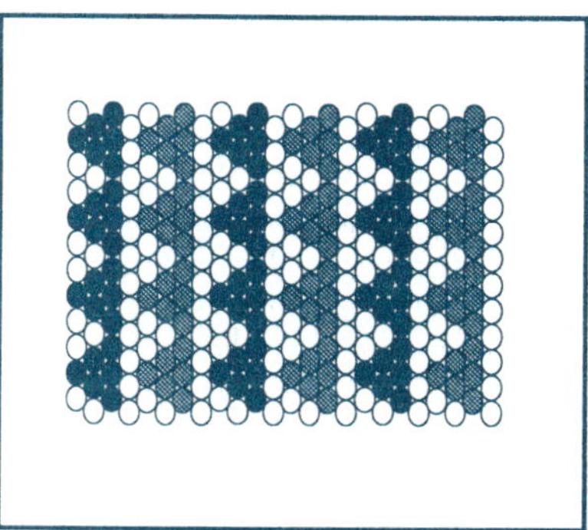

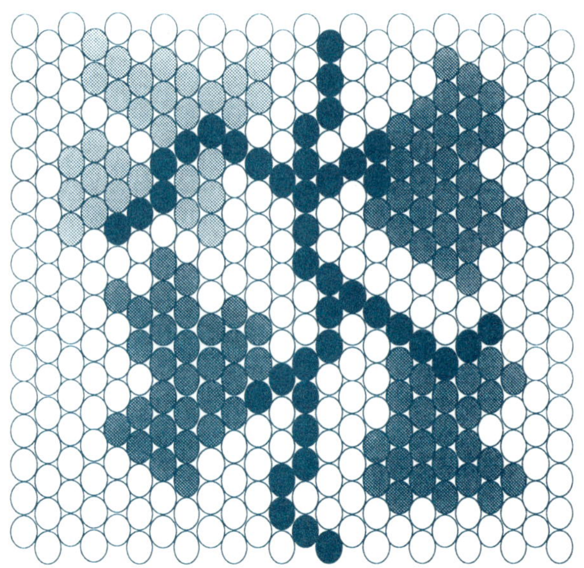

Pattern No. 25
Grape Leaves

Multiple - 24
Repeat - 32 rows

Colors
L = Light
ML = Medium Light
M = Medium
D = Dark

<u>Beginning Row (Rows 1 & 2)</u>
10L, 1D, 9L, 1ML, 3L

Row 3> 2L, 2ML, 1L, 1ML, 3L, 1M, 2L

Row 4< 2L, 1M, 2L, 1D, 1L, 4ML, 1L

Row 5> 2L, 4ML, 3L, 2M, 1L

Row 6< 2L, 2M, 1L, 1D, 1L, 3ML, 2L

Row 7> 3L, 1ML, 1D, 1L, 1D, 1L, 3M, 1L

Row 8< 2L, 2M, 1D, 2L, 2D, 1L, 1ML, 1L

Row 9> 1L, 2ML, 1D, 1ML, 3D, 2M, 2L

Row 10< 2L, 2M, 3D, 1L, 3ML, 1L

Row 11> 1L, 2ML, 1D, 1ML, 1L, 1D, 1L, 3M, 1L

Row 12< 1L, 4M, 3L, 1ML, 1D, 1ML, 1L

Row 13> 1L, 1ML, 1D, 1L, 1ML, 1L, 1D, 1L, 3M, 1L

Row 14< 2L, 2M, 8L

Row 15> 3L, 1M, 2L, 1D, 2L, 1M, 2L

Row 16< 2L, 1M, 2L, 1D, 2L, 1M, 3L

Row 17> 2L, 2M, 3L, 1D, 4L

Row 18< 4L, 2D. 1L, 3M, 2L

Row 19> 3L, 3M, 2L, 1D, 1L, 1D, 1L

Row 20< 2L, 2D, 1L, 1D, 1L, 3M, 2L

Row 21> 3L, 3M, 1D, 1L, 1M, 1D, 1M, 1L

Row 22< 1L, 3M, 2L, 1D, 2M, 3L

Row 23> 3L, 2M, 2D, 1L, 3M, 1L

Row 24< 2L, 2M, 3L, 3M, 2L

Pattern No. 25, Cont'd.

Row 25> 2L, 3M, 1L, 1D, 1L, 2M, 2L

Row 26< 2L, 3M, 3L, 2M, 2L

Row 27> 3L, 1M, 2L, 1D, 1L, 3M, 1L

Row 28< 1L, 4M, 1L, 1D, 1L, 1M, 3L

Row 29> 8L, 3M, 1L

Row 30< 6L, 1D, 5L

Row 31> 6L, 1D, 5L

Row 32< 5L, 1D, 6L

If you wish to continue with further repeats of the pattern,
do Rows 1 & 2 below, then continue with Row 3 above.

Row 1> 12L

Row 2< 5L, 1D, 4L, 1ML, 1L

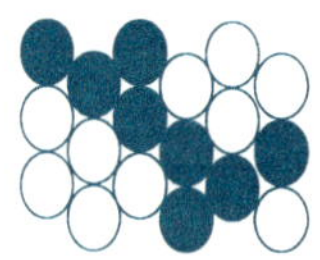

3L, 3D

Row 3> 1L, 1D, 1L

Row 4< 2D, 1L

Row 5> 2L, 1D

Row 6< 1L, 1D, 1L

If you wish to continue with further repeats
of the pattern, do Rows 1 & 2 below,
then continue with Row 3 above.

Row 1> 2D, 1L

Row 2< 2L, 1D

Pattern No. 26
Braiding

Multiple - 6
Repeat - 6 rows

Colors
L = Light
D = Dark

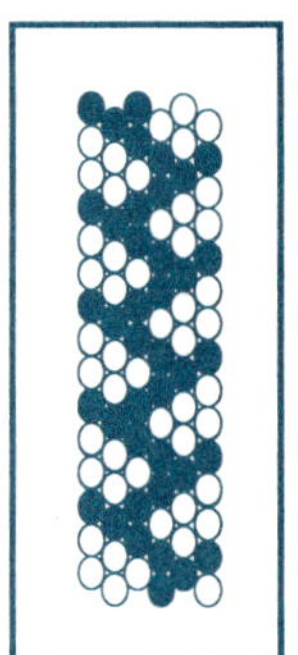

<u>Beginning Row (Rows 1 & 2)</u>
10L

Row 3> 1D, 4L

Row 4< 5L

Row 5> 1D, 4L

Row 6< 5L

Row 7> 1D, 4L

Row 8< 5L

Row 9> 1D, 4L

Row 10< 5L

Row 11>1D, 4L

Row 12< 5L

Row 13> 1D, 4L

Row 14< 4L, 1D

Row 15> 1D, 4L

Row 16< 4L, 1D

Row 17> 1D, 4L

Row 18< 4L, 1D

Row 19> 2D, 3L

Row 20< 4L, 1D

Row 21> 2D, 3L

Row 22< 4L, 1D

Row 23> 2D, 3L

Row 24< 4L, 1D

Row 25> 2D, 3L

Row 26< 4L, 1D

Row 27> 2D, 1L, 1D, 1L

Row 28< 4L, 1D

Row 29> 2D, 1L, 1D, 1L

Row 30< 3L, 2D

Row 31> 2D, 1L, 1D, 1L

Row 32< 3L, 2D

Row 33> 2D, 1L, 1D, 1L

Row 34< 1L, 1D, 1L, 2D

Row 35> 4D, 1L

Row 36< 1L, 1D, 1L, 2D

Row 37> 4D, 1L

Row 38< 1L, 1D, 1L, 2D

Row 39> 4D, 1L

Row 40< 1L, 1D, 1L, 2D

Row 41> 4D, 1L

Row 42< 1L, 1D, 1L, 2D

Row 43> 4D, 1L

Row 44< 1L, 4D

Row 45> 5D

Row 46< 1L, 4D

Row 47> 5D

Row 48< 1L, 4D

Row 49> 5D

Row 50< 1L, 4D

Row 51> 5D

Row 52< 5D

Row 53> 5D

Row 54< 5D

Row 55> 5D

Row 56< 5D

Row 57> 5D

Row 58< 5D

Row 59> 5D

Row 60< 5D

If you wish to continue with further repeats of the pattern, do Rows 1 & 2 below, then continue with Row 3 above.

Row 1> 5D

Row 2< 5D

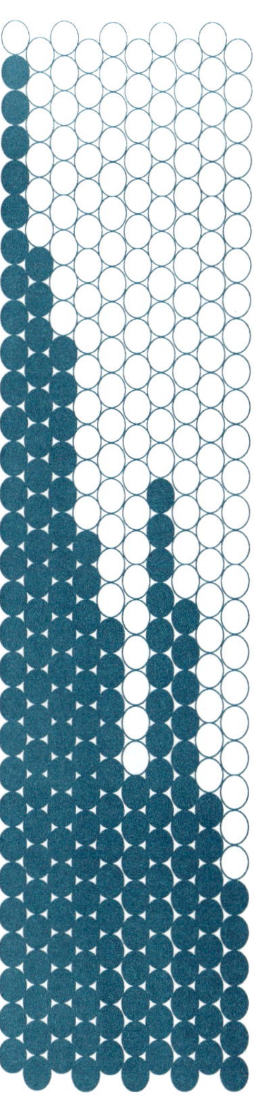

Multiple - 10
Repeat - 60 rows

Colors
L = Light
D = Dark

Pattern No. 27
Icicles

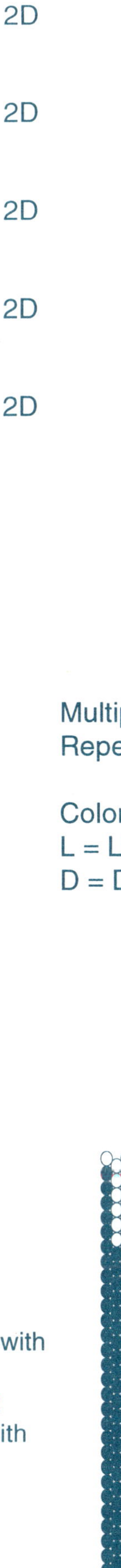

Pattern No. 28
Cosmic Chorus Line

Multiple -24
Repeat - 20 rows

Colors
L = Light
M = Medium
D = Dark

<u>Beginning Row (Rows 1 & 2)</u>
8L, 1M, 7L, 1M, 7L

Row 3> 1L, 1D, 1L, 1M, 4L, 1M, 1L, 1D, 1L

Row 4< 2L, 1D, 2M, 3L, 2M, 1D, 1L

Row 5> 1L, 2D, 1M, 4L, 1M, 2D, 1L

Row 6< 2L, 1D, 1L, 1M, 3L, 1M, 1L, 1D, 1L

Row 7> 1L, 1D, (2L, 1D X 3), 1L

Row 8< 5L, 1D, 1L, 1D, 4L

Row 9> 1L, 1M, 2L, 4D, 2L, 1M, 1L

Row 10< 1L, 1M, 3L, 1D, 1L, 1D, 3L, 1M

Row 11> 2M, 2L, 1D, 2L, 1D, 2L, 2M

Row 12< 1L, 1M, 9L, 1M

Row 13> 1L, 1M, (2L, 1M X 3), 1L

Row 14< 2L, 1D, 1L, 1M, 3L, 1M, 1L, 1D, 1L

Row 15> 2L, 1D, 2M, 2L, 2M, 1D, 2L

Row 16< 2L, 2D, 1M, 3L, 1M, 2D, 1L

Row 17> 2L, 1D, 1L, 1M, 2L, 1M, 1L, 1D, 2L

Row 18< 2L, 1D, 7L, 1D, 1L

Row 19> 12L

Row 20< 12L

If you wish to continue with further repeats of the pattern, do Rows 1 & 2 below, then continue with Row 3 above.

Row 1> 12L

Row 2< 4L, 1M, 3L, 1M, 3L

<u>Beginning Row (Rows 1 & 2)</u>
3L, 2D, 4L, 2D, 1L

Row 3> 6D

Row 4< 6L

Row 5> 1L, 2D, 1L, 2D

Row 6< 1L, 2D, 1L, 2D

Row 7> 1D, 1L, 2D, 1L, 1D

Row 8< 1M, 1L, 1D, 1M, 1L, 1D

Row 9> 1L, 1D, 2L, 1D, 1L

Row 10< 1D, 2L, 1D, 2L

Row 11> 2L, 1D, 2L, 1D

Row 12< 6D

Row 13> 6L

Row 14< 1D, 1L, 2D, 1L, 1D

Row 15> 1D, 1L, 2D, 1L, 1D

Row 16< 1L, 2D, 1L, 2D

Row 17> 1L, 1M, 1D, 1L, 1M, 1D

Row 18< 1D, 2L, 1D, 2L

If you wish to continue with further repeats of the
pattern, do Rows 1 & 2 below, then continue with
Row 3 above.

Row 1> 1L, 1D, 2L, 1D, 1L

Row 2< 2L, 1D, 2L, 1D

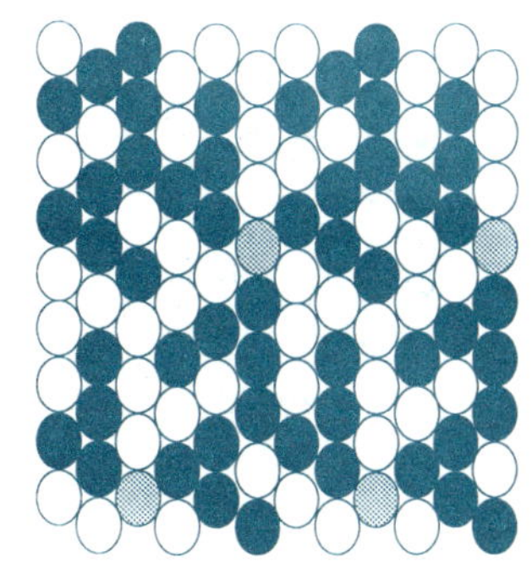

Pattern No. 29
Escher's Wiggles

Multiple - 12
Repeat - 18 rows

Colors
L = Light
M = Medium
D = Dark

Pattern No. 30
Perky Pansy

Multiple - 10
Repeat - 24 rows

Colors
L = Light
ML = Medium light
M = Medium
G = Green
D = Dark

2L, 3D, 5L

Row 3> 3L, 1M, 1D

Row 4< 1D, 1M, 1D, 2L

Row 5> 1L, 1D, 1L, 1ML, 1M

Row 6< 1L, 1ML, 1D, 1M, 1L

Row 7> 1L, 1D, 2ML, 1L

Row 8< 1L, 1D, 1ML, 1M, 1L

Row 9> 1L, 1D, 2ML, 1D

Row 10< 1D, 1ML, 1D, 1M, 1L

Row 11> 1L, 2D, 1ML, 1M

Row 12< 1D, 1M, 1L, 1D, 1L

Row 13> 3L, 1M, 1D

Row 14< 1L, 1D, 1G, 2L

Row 15> 2L, 1G, 1D, 1L

Row 16< 5L

Row 17> 2L, 1G, 2L

Row 18< 4L, 1G

Row 19> 1L, 2G, 2L

Row 20< 4L, 1G

Row 21> 1L, 2G, 2L

Row 22< 3L, 1G, 1L

Row 23> 2L, 1G, 2L

Row 24< 5L

If you wish to continue with further repeats of the pattern, do Rows 1 & 2 below, then continue with Row 3 above.

Row 1> 3L, 1D, 1L

Row 2< 1L, 2D, 2L

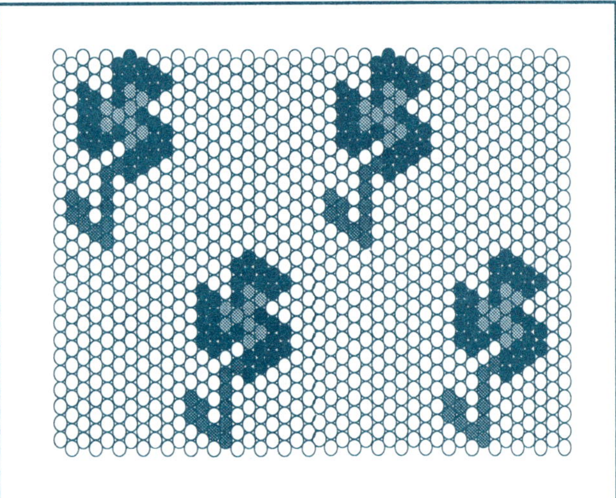

20L, 2MD

Row 3> 2MD, 3L, 3MD, 3L

Row 4< 3L, 4MD, 2L, 2MD

Row 5> 3MD, 2L, 4MD, 2L

Row 6< 2L, 5MD, 1X, 3MD

Row 7> 3MD, 2L, 4MD, 2L

Row 8< 2L, 5MD, 1X, 3MD

Row 9> 3MD, 2L, 4MD, 2L

Row 10< 2L, 5MD, 1X, 3MD

Row 11> 3MD, 2L, 4MD, 2L

Row 12< 2L, 5MD, 1X, 3MD

Row 13> 3MD, 2L, 4MD, 2L

Row 14< 2L, 4MD, 1L, 1X, 3MD

Row 15> 3MD, 1L, 1X, 1L, 3MD, 2L

Row 16< 2L, 3MD, 1L, 1X, 1L, 3MD

Row 17> 4MD, 1L, 1X, 1L, 2MD, 2L

Row 18< 3L, 1MD, 1L, 1X, 1L, 4MD

Pattern No. 31
Pinafore Girl

Multiple - 22
Repeat - 74 rows

Colors
L = Light
ML = Medium Light
M = Medium
MD = Medium Dark
D = Dark
X = Accent

Row 19> 1L, 4MD, 1L, 1X, 5L

Row 20< 4L, 1X, 1L, 4MD, 1L

Row 21> 2L, 4MD, 5L

Row 22< 5L, 1MD, 2ML, 1MD, 2L

Row 23> 4L, 3ML, 4L

Row 24< 4L, 4ML, 3L

Row 25> 3L, 5ML, 3L

Row 26< 3L, 2ML, 1M, 2ML, 3L

Row 27> 3L, 2ML, 2M, 2ML, 2L

Row 28< 3L, 1ML, 3M, 1ML, 3L

Row 29> 3L, 2ML, 3M, 1ML, 2L

Row 30< 3L, 1ML, 3M, 2ML, 2L

Row 31> 3L, 2ML, 3M, 1ML, 2L

Row 30< 3L, 1ML, 3M, 2ML, 2L

Row 33> 3L, 2ML, 3M, 1ML, 2L

Row 34< 3L, 1ML, 3M, 2ML, 2L

Row 35> 2L, 3ML, 3M, 1ML, 2L

Row 36< 2L, 2ML, 2M, 3ML, 2L

Row 37> 2L, 3ML, 3M, 1ML, 2L

Row 38< 2L, 2ML, 2M, 3ML, 2L

Row 39> 2L, 3ML, 3M, 1ML, 2L

Row 40< 2L, 2ML, 3M, 2ML, 2L

Row 41> 2L, 2ML, 1L, 3M, 2ML, 1L

Row 42< 2L, 2ML, 2M, 1L, 1X, 2ML, 1L

Row 43> 2L, 1ML, 1L, 1X, 1L, 1M, 3ML, 1L

Row 44< 1L, 4ML, 1L, 1X, 1L, 2ML, 1L

Row 45> 1L, 3ML, 1L, 1X, 4ML, 1L

Row 46< 1L, 5ML, 1L, 3ML, 1L

Row 47> 1L, 9ML, 1L

Row 48< 1L, 9ML, 1L

Row 49> 1L, 10ML

Row 50< 11ML

Row 51> 1L, 10ML

Row 50< 11ML

Row 53> 11ML

Row 54< 11ML

Row 55> 11ML

Row 56< 11ML

Row 57> 11MD

Row 58< 11MD

Row 59> 11MD

Row 60< 11MD

Row 61> 11MD

Row 62< 11MD

Row 63> 4L, 3D, 4L

Row 64< 4L, 3D, 4L

Row 65> 4L, 3D, 4L

Row 66< 4L, 3D, 4L

Row 67> 4L, 3D, 4L

Row 68< 4L, 4D, 3L

Row 69> 3L, 4D, 4L

Row 70< 4L, 5D, 2L

Row 671> 3L, 4D, 4L

Row 72< 5L, 1D, 1L, 1D, 3L

Row 73> 11L

Row 74< 11L

If you wish to continue with further repeats of the pattern, do Rows 1 & 2 below, then continue with Row 3 above.

Row 1> 1MD, 10L

Row 2< 10L, 1MD

<u>Beginning Row (Rows 1 & 2)</u>
1D, 9L, 2D

Row 3> 1M, 1D, 3L, 1D

Row 4< 1M, 1D, 2L, 1D, 1M

Row 5> 1M, 1D, 3L, 1D

Row 6< 1D, 4L, 1D

Row 7> 1D, 1ML, 3L, 1ML

Row 8< 1D, 1ML, 2L, 1ML, 1D

Row 9> 1L, 1D, 1ML, 1L, 1ML, 1D

Row 10< 1L, 1D, 2ML, 1D, 1L

Row 11> 2L, 1D, 1ML, 1D, 1L

Row 12< 2L, 2D, 2L

Row 13> 3L, 1D, 2L

Row 14< 6L

If you wish to continue with further repeats of the
pattern, do Rows 1 & 2 below, then continue with
Row 3 above.

Row 1> 1D, 5L

Row 2< 1D, 4L, 1D

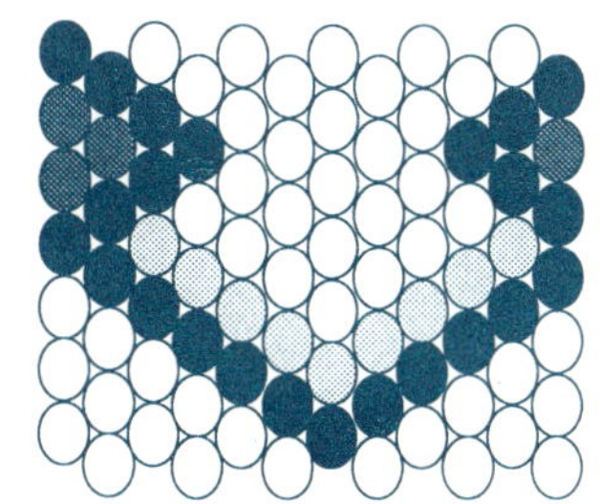

Pattern No. 32
Loop de loop

Multiple - 12
Repeat - 14 rows

Colors
L = Light
M = Medium
D = Dark

Pattern No. 33
Fans & Butterflies

Multiple - 30
Repeat - 42 rows

Colors
L = Light
D = Dark

<u>Beginning Row (Rows 1 & 2)</u>
4L, 1D, 5L, 1D, 2L, 5D, 2L, 1D, 5L, 1D, 3L

Row 3> (1L, 2D X 2), 1L, 1D, 1L, (2D, 1L X 2)

Row 4< 1L, 1D, 1L, 2D, 1L, 1D, 2L, 1D, 1L, 2D, 1L, 1D

Row 5> (1D, 2L X 2), 1D, 1L, (1D, 2L X 2), 1D

Row 6< 1L, 1D, 12L, 1D

Row 7> 1L, (1D, 5L X2), 1D, 1L

Row 8< 2L, 1D, 4L, 2D, 4L, 1D, 1L

Row 9> 2L, 1D, 3L, 1D, 1L, 1D, 3L, 1D, 2L

Row 10< 3L, (1D, 2L X 4)

Row 11> 3L, (1D, 1L X 4), 1D, 3L

Row 12< 4L, 1D, 1L, 1D, 2L, 1D, 1L, 1D, 3L

Row 13> 4L, (1D, 1L X 3), 1D, 4L

Row 14< 5L, 1D, 1L, 2D, 1L, 1D, 4L

Row 15> 1L, 1D, 3L, (1D, 1L X 2), 1D, 3L, 1D, 1L

Row 16< 1L, 1D, 4L, 1D, 2L, 1D, 4L, 1D

Row 17> 1D, (2L, 1D X 2), 1L, 1D, (2L, 1D X 2)

Row 18< 1L, 1D, 1L, 2D, 1L, 1D, 2L, 1D, 1L, 2D, 1L, 1D

Row 19> (1L, 2D X 2), 1L, 1D, (1L, 2D X 2),1L

Row 20< (2L, 1D X 2), 1L, 2D, 1L, 1D, 2L, 1D, 1L

Pattern No. 33, con't.

Row 21> 6L, 3D, 6L

Row 22< 6L, 4D, 5L

Row 23> 6L, 3D, 6L

Row 24< (2L, 1D X2), 1L, 2D, 1L, 1D, 2L, 1D, 1L

Row 25> (1L, 2D X 2), 1L, 1D, (1L, 2D X 2), 1L

Row 26< 1L, 1D, 1L, 2D, 1L, 1D, 2L, 1D, 1L, 2D, 1L, 1D

Row 27> 1D, 2L, 1D, 2L, 1D, 1L, 1D, 2L, 1D, 2L, 1D

Row 28< 1L, 1D, 4L, 1D, 2L, 1D, 4L, 1D

Row 29> 1L, 1D, 3L, (1D, 1L X 2), 1D, 3L, 1D, 1L

Row 30< 5L, 1D, 1L, 2D, 1L, 1D, 4L

Row 31> 4L, (1D, 1L X 4), 3L

Row 32< 4L, 1D, 1L, 1D, 2L, 1D, 1L, 1D, 3L

Row 33> 3L, (1D, 1L X 5), 2L

Row 34< 3L, (1D, 2L X 4)

Row 35> 2L, 1D, 3L, 1D, 1L, 1D, 3L, 1D, 2L

Row 36< 2L, 1D, 4L, 2D, 4L, 1D, 1L

Row 37> 1L, 1D, 3L, 1D, 1L, 1D, 1L, 1D, 3L, 1D, 1L

Row 38< 1L, 1D, 4L, 1D, 2L, 1D, 4L, 1D

Row 39> (1D, 2L X 2), 1D, 1L, 1D, (2L, 1D X 2)

Row 40< 1L, 1D, 1L, 2D, 1L, 1D, 2L, 1D, lL, 2D, 1L, 1D

Row 41> (1L, 2D X 2), 1L, 1D, (1L, 2D X 2), 1L

Row 42< (2L, 1D X 2),1L, 2D, 1L, 1D, 2L, 1D, 1L

If you wish to continue with further repeats of the pattern,
do Rows 1 & 2 below, then continue with Row 3 above.

Row 1> 6L, 3D, 6L

Row 2< (2L, 1D X 2), 1L, 2D, 1L, 1D, 2L, 1D, 1L

Pattern No. 34
Endless Knot

Multiple - 42
Repeat - 30 rows

Colors
L = Light
D = Dark

Row 7> (1L, 1D X 10), 1L

Row 8< (1L, 1D X 2), 2L, 1D, 1L, 2D, 2L, 1D,
1L, 2D, 2L, 1D, 1L, 1D

Row 9> (1D, 1L, 1D, 3L X 3), 1D, 1L, 1D

Row 10< 1L, 1D, (1L, 1D, 2L, 2D X 2), 1L,
1D, 2L, 1D, 1L, 1D

Row 11> (1L, 1D X 10), 1L

Row 12< 2L, 1D, (1L, 2D X 5), 1L, 1D, 1L

Row 13> 2L, (1D, 1L X 9), 1L

Row 14< 3L, 2D, 1L, 1D, 2L, 2D, 1L, 1D, 2L,
2D, 1L, 1D, 2L

Row 15> 3L, (1D, 1L, 1D, 3L X 3)

Row 16< 3L, 1D, 1L, 2D, 2L, 1D, 1L, 2D, 2L,
1D, 1L, 2D, 2L

Row 17> 2L, (1D, 1L X 9), 1L

Row 18< 2L, 1D, (1L, 2D X 5), 1L, 1D, 1L

Row 19> (1L, 1D X 10), 1L

Row 20< (1L, 1D X 2), 2L, 1D, 1L, 2D, 2L, 1D, 1L, 2D, 2L, 1D, 1L, 1D

Row 21> (1D, 1L, 1D, 3L X 3), 1D, 1L, 1D

Row 22< (1L, 1D X 2), 2L, 2D, 1L, 1D, 2L, 2D, 1L, 1D, 2L, 1D, 1L, 1D

Row 23> (1L, 1D X 10), 1L

Row 24< 2L, 1D, (1L, 2D X 5), 1L, 1D, 1L

Row 25> 2L, (1D, 1L X 9), 1L

Row 26< 3L, (1D, 2L X 6)

Row 27> (3L, 1D, 1L, 1D X 3), 3L

Row 28< (4L, 2D X 3), 3L

Row 29> 4L, (1D, 5L X 2), 1D, 4L

Row 30< 21L

If you wish to continue with further repeats of the pattern, do Rows 1 & 2 below, then continue with Row 3 above.

Row 1> 4L, (1D, 5L X 2), 1D, 4L

Row 2< (4L, 2D X 3), 3L

Pattern No. 35
Piano Keys

Multiple - 24
Repeat - 38 rows

Colors
L = Light
D = Dark

<u>Beginning Row (Rows 1 & 2)</u>
2L, (1L, 3D X 3), 3L, 3D, 1L, 3D

Odd-numbered Rows 3-21> 4D, 1L, 6D, 1L

Even-numbered Rows 4-20< 2L, 1D, (1L, 1D X 2), 2L, 1D, 1L, 1D

Row 22< 2L, (1D, 1L X 3), (1L, 1D X 2)

Rows 23-36: 12L
(For the piano key effect, repeat the pattern across, but not down. In other words, make the piece wider, but not longer.)

If you wish to continue with further repeats of the pattern, do Rows 1 & 2 below, then continue with Row 3 above.

Row 1> 4D, 1L, 6D, 1L

Row 2< 2L, (1D, 1L,) x 3, (1L, 1D) x 2

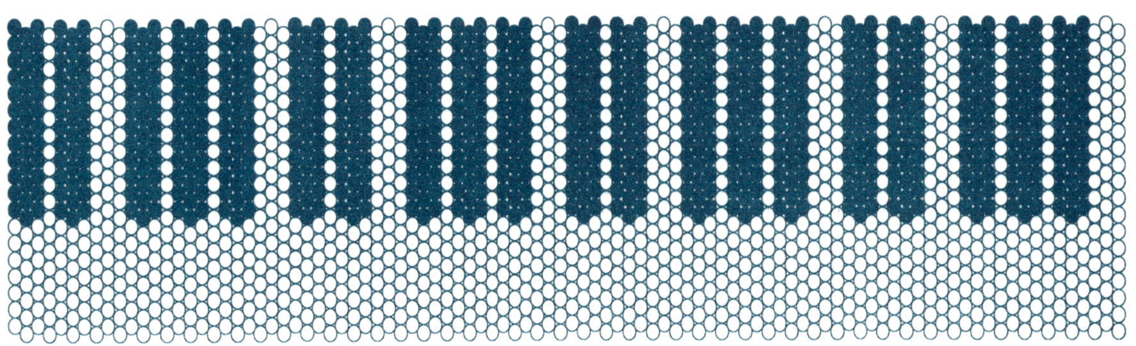

<u>Beginning Row (Rows 1 & 2)</u>
17L, 1D, 16L

Row 3> 8L, 1D, 8L

Row 4< 17L

Row 5> 6L, 1D, 1L, 1D, 1L, 1D, 6L

Row 6< 7L, 1D, 2L, 1D, 6L

Row 7> 7L, 3D, 7L

Row 8< 8L, 2D, 7L

Row 9> 8L, 1D, 8L

Row 10< 17L

Row 11> 8L, 1D, 8L

Row 12< 17L

Row 13> 7L, 3D, 7L

Row 14< 8L, 2D, 7L

Row 15> (2L, 1D X 5), 2L

Row 16< 6L, 1D, 4L, 1D, 5L

Pattern No. 36
Snowflake

Multiple - 34
Repeat - 68 rows

Colors
L = Light
D = Dark

Pattern No. 36, con't.

Row 17> 1D, 1L, 1D, 2L, 2D, 1L, 1D, 1L, 2D, 2L, 1D, 1L, 1D

Row 18< 1L, 1D, 5L, 1D, 2L, 1D, 5L, 1D

Row 19> 1L, 2D, 2L, 1D, 1L, 3D, 1L, 1D, 2L, 2D, 1L

Row 20< 2L, 1D, 1L, 1D, 3L, 2D, 3L, 1D, 1L, 1D, 1L

Row 21> (2L, 1D X 5), 2L

Row 22< 2L, 3D, 8L, 3D, 1L

Row 23> (1L, 1D X 3), 3D, (1L, 1D X 3), 1L

Row 24< 1L, 1D, 2L, 1D, 3L, 2D, 3L, 1D, 2L, 1D

Row 25> 3L, 4D, 1L, 1D, 1L, 4D, 3L

Row 26< 3L, 1D, 1L, 1D, 6L, 1D, 1L, 1D, 2L

Row 27> 5L, 2D, 1L, 1D, 1L, 2D, 5L

Row 28< 5L, 2D, 4L, 2D, 4L

Row 29> 4L, (1D, 1L X 5), 3L

Row 30< 4L, 1D, 1L, 2D, 2L, 2D, 1L, 1D, 3L

Row 31> 3L, (1D, 1L X 2), 3D, (1L, 1D X 2), 3L

Row 32< 3L, 1D, 4L, 2D, 4L, 1D, 2L

Row 33> 2L, 1D, 5L, 1D, 5L, 1D, 2L

Row 34< 3L, 1D, 4L, 2D, 4L, 1D, 2L

Row 35> 3L, (1D, 1L X 2), 3D, (1L, 1D X 2), 3L

Row 36< 4L, 1D, 1L, 2D, 2L, 2D, 1L, 1D, 3L

Row 37> 4L, (1D, 1L X 5)3L

Row 38< 5L, 2D, 4L, 2D, 4L

Row 39> 5L, 2D, 1L, 1D, 1L, 2D, 5L

Row 40< 3L, 1D, 1L, 1D, 6L, 1D, 1L, 1D, 2L

Row 41> 3L, 4D, 1L, 1D, 1L, 4D, 3L

Row 42< 1L, 1D, 2L, 1D, 3L, 2D, 3L, 1D, 2L, 1D

Row 43> (1L, 1D X 3), 1L, 3D, (1L, 1D X 3), 1L

Row 44< 2L, 3D, 8L, 3D, 1L

Row 45> (2L, 1D X 5), 2L

Row 46< 2L, 1D, 1L, 1D, 3L, 2D, 3L, (1D, 1L X 2)

Row 47> 1L, 2D, 2L, 1D, 1L, 3D, 1L, 1D, 2L, 2D, 1L

Row 48< 1L, 1D, 5L, 1D, 2L, 1D, 5L, 1D

Row 49> 1D, 1L, 1D, 2L, 2D, 1L, 1D, 1L, 2D, 2L, 1D, 1L, 1D

Row 50< 6L, 1D, 4L, 1D, 5L

Row 51> (2L, 1D X 5), 2L

Row 52< 8L, 2D, 7L

Row 53> 7L, 3D, 7L

Row 54< 17L

Row 55> 8L, 1D, 8L

Row 56< 17L

Row 57> 8L, 1D, 8L

Row 58< 8L, 2D, 7L

Row 59> 7L, 3D, 7L

Row 60< 7L, 1D, 2L, 1D, 6L

Row 61> 8L, 1D, 8L

Row 62< 17L

Row 63> 8L, 1D, 8L

Row 64< 17L

Row 65> 8L, 1D, 8L

Row 66< 17L

Row 67> 17L

Row 68< 17L

If you wish to continue with **further repeats of the pattern**, do Rows 1 & 2 below, then continue with Row 3 above.

Row 1> 8L, 1D, 8L

Row 2< 17L

<u>Beginning Row (Rows 1 & 2)</u>
8D

Row 3> 4D

Row 4< 4D

Row 5> 2D, 1L, 1D

Row 6< 2D, 1L, 1D

Row 7> 1D, 2L, 1D

Row 8< 2D, 2L

Row 9> 3L, 1D

Row 10< 1L, 1D, 2L

Row 11> 1L, 1D, 2L

Row 12< 3L, 1D

Row 13> 2D, 2L

Row 14< 1D, 2L, 1D

Row 15> 2D, 1L, 1D

Row 16< 2D, 1L, 1D

Row 17> 4D

Row 18< 4D

If you wish to continue with further repeats of the pattern, do Rows 1 & 2 below, then continue with Row 3 above.

Row 1> 4D

Row 2< 4D

Pattern No. 37
Lightning

Multiple - 8
Repeat - 18 rows

Colors
L = Light
D = Dark

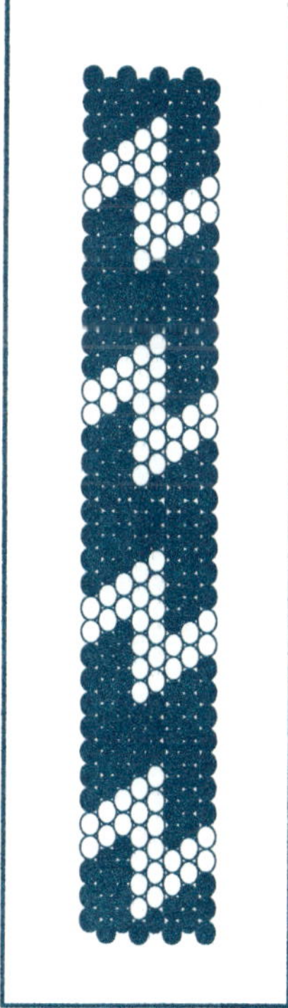

Pattern No. 38
Crown Jewels

Multiple - 10
Repeat - 28 rows

Colors
L = Light
M = Medium
D = Dark

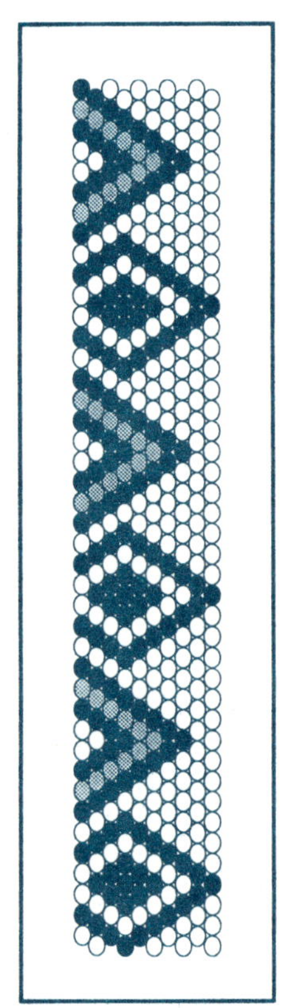

<u>Beginning Row (Rows 1 & 2)</u>
8L, 2D

Row 3> 1M, 1D, 3L

Row 4< 3L, 1D, 1M

Row 5> 1D, 1M, 1D, 2L

Row 6< 2L, 1D, 1M, 1D

Row 7> 1L, 1D, 1M, 1D, 1L

Row 8< 1L, 1D, 1M, 1D, 1L

Row 9> 1L, 1D, 1M, 1D, 1L

Row 10< 2L, 1D, 1M, 1D

Row 11> 1D, 1M, 1D, 2L

Row 12< 3L, 1D, 1M

Row 13> 1M, 1D, 3L

Row 14< 4L, 1D

Row 15> 1D, 4L

Row 16< 3L, 1D, 1L

Row 17> 1L, 2D, 2L

Row 18< 2L, 1D, 1L, 1D

Row 19> 1D, 2L, 1D, 1L

Row 20< (1L, 1D X 2), 1L

Row 21> 1L, 2D, 1L, 1D

Row 22< 1D, 1L, 3D

Row 23> 1L, 2D, 1L, 1D

Row 24< (1L, 1D X 2), 1L

Row 25> 1D, 2L, 1D, 1L

Row 26< 2L, 1D, 1L, 1D

Row 27> 1L, 2D, 2L

Row 28< 3L, 1D, 1L

If you wish to continue with further repeats of the pattern, do Rows 1 & 2 below, then continue with Row 3 above.

Row 1> 1D, 4L

Row 2< 4L, 1D

4D, 2L

Row 3> 1D, 1L, 1D

Row 4< 1D, 1L, 1D

Row 5> 2D, 1L

Row 6< 1L, 2D

Row 7> 2D, 1L

Row 8< 1D, 1L, 1D

Row 9> 1D, 1L, 1D

Row 10< 2D, 1L

If you wish to continue with further repeats of the
pattern, do Rows 1 & 2 below, then continue with
Row 3 above.

Row 1> 1L, 2D

Row 2< 2D, 1L

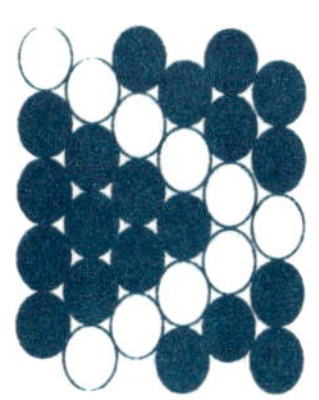

Pattern No. 39
Zig Zag

Multiple - 6
Repeat - 10 rows

Colors
L = Light
D = Dark

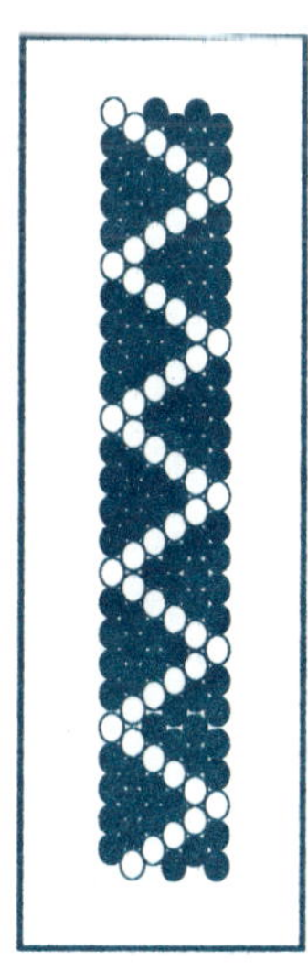

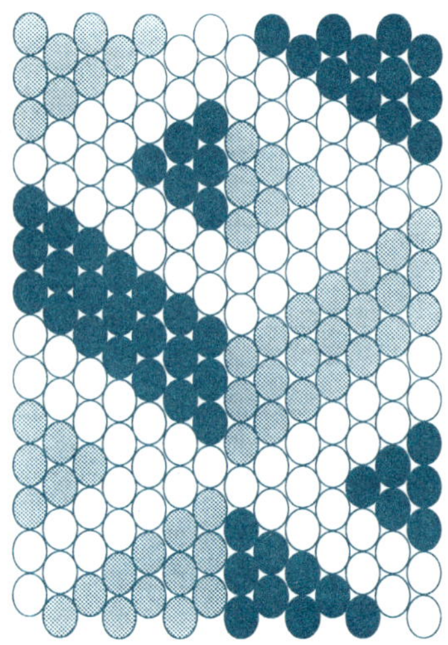

Pattern No. 40
Boxes

Multiple - 14
Repeat - 28 rows

Colors
L = Light
M = Medium
D = Dark

<u>Beginning Row (Rows 1 & 2)</u>
6D, 3L, 5M

Row 3> 2M, 3L, 2D

Row 4< 2D, 4L, 1M

Row 5> 1M, 2L, 1D, 2L, 1D

Row 6< 1D, 2L, 1M, 1D, 2L

Row 7> 2L, 2D, 1M, 2L

Row 8< 2L, 2M, 1D, 2L

Row 9> 1D, 2L, 1D, 1M, 2L

Row 10< 1M, 2L, 1M, 2L, 1D

Row 1> 2D, 4L, 1M

Row 12< 2M, 3L, 2D

Row 13> 3D, 2L, 2M

Row 14< 3M, 1L, 3D

Row 15> 1L, 3D, 3M

Row 16< 1L, 3M, 2D, 1L

Row 17> 2L, 2D, 2M, 1L

Row 18< 2L, 2M, 1D, 2L

Row 19> 1M, 2L, 1D, 1M, 2L

Row 20< 1D, 2L, 1M, 2L, 1M

Row 21> 2M, 4L, 1D

Row 22< 2D, 4L, 1M

Row 23> 1M, 2L, 1M, 2L, 1D

Row 24< 1D, 2L, 1D, 1M, 2L

Row 25> 2L, 2M, 1D, 2L

Row 26< 2L, 2D, 2M, 1L

Row 27> 1L, 3M, 2D, 1L

Row 28< 1L, 3D, 3M

If you wish to continue with further repeats of the pattern, do Rows 1 & 2 below, then continue with Row 3 above.

Row 1> 3M, 1L, 3D

Row 2< 3D, 2L, 2M

<u>Beginning Row (Rows 1 & 2)</u>
13L, 2D, 3L, 2D

Row 3> 4D, 6L

Row 4< 3L, 1D, 3L, 1D, 1L, 1D

Row 5> 1D, 2L, 1D, 6L

Row 6< 10L

Row 7> 10L

Row 8< 3L, 1D, 4L, 1D, 1L

Row 9> 10L

Row 10< 10L

Row 11> 5L, 1D, 2L, 1D, 1L

Row 12< 2L, 1D, 1L, 1D, 3L, 1D, 1L

Row 13> 5L, 4D, 1L

Row 14< 2L, 1D, 1L, 1D, 5L

Row 15> 5L, 1D, 2L, 1D, 1L

Row 16< 8L, 1D, 1L

Row 17> 10L

Row 18< 3L, 1D, 6L

It you wish to continue with further repeats of the
pattern, do Rows 1 & 2 below, then continue with
Row 3 above.

Row 1> 1D, 2L, 1D, 6L

Row 2< 7L, 1D, 1L, 1D

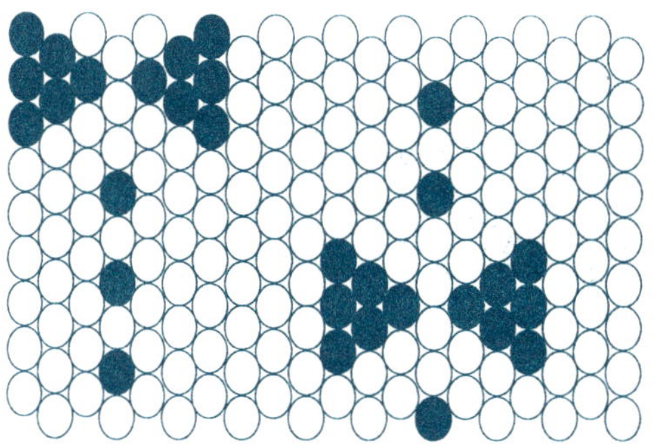

Pattern No. 41
Buttons 'n Bows

Multiple - 20
Repeat - 18 rows

Colors
L = Light
D = Dark

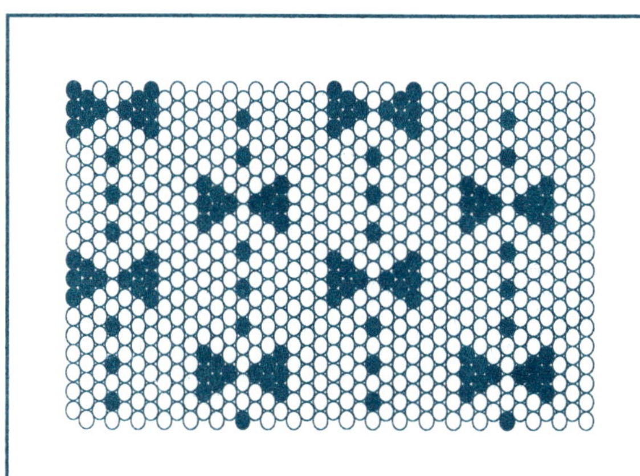

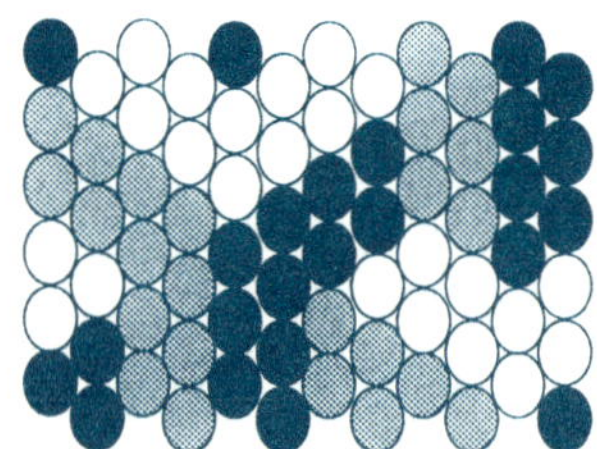

Pattern No. 42
Stacking Tees

Multiple - 12
Repeat - 12 rows

Colors
L = Light
M = Medium
D = Dark

<u>Beginning Row (Rows 1 & 2)</u>
2D, 2M, (3L, 1D X 2)

Row 3> 1M, 3L, 1M, 1D

Row 4< 1D, 1M, 1D, 2L, 1M

Row 5> 2M, 1L, 1D, 1M, 1D

Row 6< 1D, 1M, 2D, 2M

Row 7> 1L, 1M, 2D, 1L, 1D

Row 8< 3L, 1D, 1M, 1L

Row 9> 1L, 1M, 1D, 1M, 2L

Row 10< 2L, 1M, 1D, 1M, 1D

Row 11> 1D, 1M, 1D, 2M, 1L

Row 12< 1D, 2M, 1D, 1M, 1D

If you wish to continue with further repeats of the pattern, do Rows 1 & 2 below, then continue with Row 3 above.

Row 1> (1D, 1L X 2),1M, 1D

Row 2< 1D, 1M, 4L

(1L, 1M X 2), 2D

Row 3> 2D, 1M

Row 4< 1L, 2D

Row 5> 2D, 1M

Row 6< 2L, 1D

Row 7> 1D, 2M

Row 8< 3L

Row 9> 3M

Row 10< 3L

Row 11> 3M

Row 12< 1D, 2L

Row 13> 2M, 1D

Row 14< 2D, 1L

Row 15> 1M, 2D

Row 16< 2D, 1L

Row 17> 2M, 1D

Row 18< 1D, 2L

Row 19> 3M

Row 20< 3L

Row 21> 3M

Row 22< 3L

If you wish to continue with further repeats of the
pattern, do Rows 1 & 2 below, then continue with
Row 3 above.

Row 1> 1D, 2M

Row 2< 2L, 1D

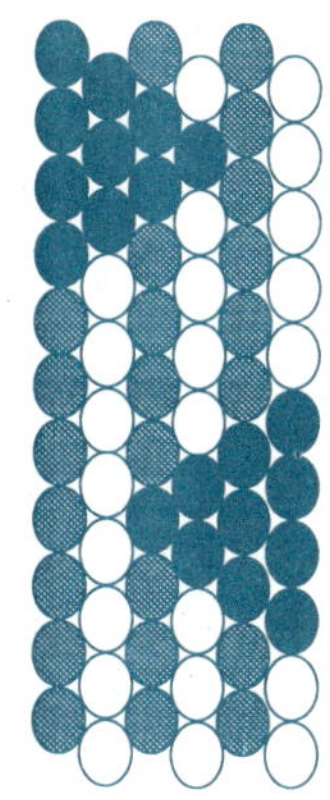

Pattern No. 43
Stripes & Triangles

Multiple - 6
Repeat - 22 rows

Colors
L = Light
M = Medium
D = Dark

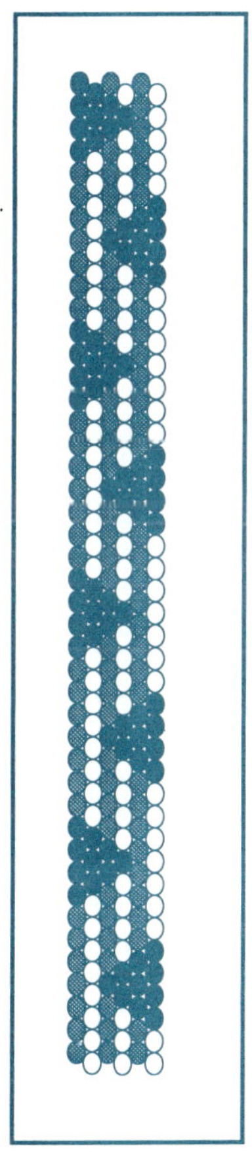

Pattern No. 44
Diamond Chain

Multiple - 8
Repeat - 24 rows

Colors
L = Light
M = Medium
D = Dark

1D, 4L, 3M

Row 3> 1M, 2L, 1D

Row 4< 2D, 1L, 1M

Row 5> 1M, 1L, 2D

Row 6< 2D, 1L, 1M

Row 7> 1M, 1L, 2D

Row 8< 2D, 1L, 1M

Row 9> 1M, 1L, 2D

Row 10< 1L, 1D, 1L, 1M

Row 11> 1M, 1L, 1D, 1L

Row 12< 3L, 1M

Row 13> 1M, 3L

Row 14< 2L, 1D, 1M

Row 15> 1M, 1D, 2L

Row 16< 2L, 2D

Row 17> 2D, 2L

Row 18< 1M, 1L, 2D

Row 19> 2D, 1L, 1M

Row 20< 2M, 2D

Row 21> 2D, 2M

Row 22< 1L, 2M, 1D

Row 23> 1D, 2M, 1L

Row 24< 2L, 2M

If you wish to continue with further repeats of the pattern, do Rows 1 & 2 below, then continue with Row 3 above.

Row 1> 2M, 2L

Row 2< 1D, 2L, 1M

Beginning Row (Rows 1 & 2)
9ML, 2L, 2M, 13ML, 1L, 9ML

Row 3> 4ML, 1M, 1L, 5ML, 2M,
1L, 4ML

Row 4< 5ML, 1L, 2M, 4ML, 2L,
1M, 3ML

Row 5> 4ML, 1M, 2L, 3ML, 2M,
2L, 4ML

Row 6< 5ML, 2L, 2M, 2ML, 3L,
1M, 3ML

Row 7> 4ML, 1M, 3L, 1ML, 2M,
3L, 4ML

Row 8< 5ML, 3L, 2M, 2L, 1D, 1L,
1M, 3ML

Row 9> 4ML, 1M, 1L, 1D, 2L,
1M, 2L, 1D, 1L, 4ML

Row 10< 5ML, 1L, 1D, 2L, 1D,
1L, 2D, 1L, 1M, 3ML

Row 11> 4ML, 1M, 1L, 2D, 1L,
1D, 1L, 1ML, 1D, 1L, 4ML

Row 12< 5ML, 1L, 1D, 1ML, 1L,
1D, 1L, 1D, 1ML, 1L, 1M, 3ML

Row 13> 4ML, 1M, 1L, 1ML, 1M,
1L, 1D, 1L, 1ML, 1D, 1L, 4ML

Row 14< 5ML, 1L, 1D, 1ML, 1L,
1D, 1L, 1M, 1ML, 1L, 1M, 3ML

Row 15> 4ML, 1M, 1L, 1ML, 1M,
1L, 1D, 1L, 1M, 1D, 1L, 4ML

Row 16< 5ML, 1L, 2M, 1L, 1D,
1L, 1M, 2L, 1M, 3ML

Row 17> 4ML, 1M, 2L, 1M, 1L,
1D, 1L, 1M, 2L, 4ML

Pattern No. 45
Twisting Star

Multiple - 36
Repeat - 56 rows

Colors
L = Light
ML = Medium Light
M = Medium
D = Dark

Row 18< 4ML, 1M, 2L, 1M, 1L, 1D, 3L, 1D, 1M, 3ML

Row 19> 4ML, 2D, 3L, 1D, 3L, 1D, 1M, 3ML

Row 20< 3ML, 2M, 1D, 3L, 1D, 2L, 2D, 1L, 3ML

Row 21> 3ML, 2L, 2D, 2L, 1D, 2L, 2D, 2M, 2ML

Row 22< 2ML, 2M, 1L, 2D, 2L, 1D, 1L, 2D, 3L, 2ML

Row 23> 2ML, 4L, 2D, 1L, 1D, 1L, 2D, 2L, 2M, 1ML

Row 24< 1ML, 2M, 3L, 2D, 1L, 3D, 2L, 1D, 2L, 1ML

Row 25> 1ML, 2L, 1D, 1M, 2L, 5D, 4L, 2M

Row 26< 1ML, 1M, 2L, 1ML, 2L, 2D, 1L, 1D, 2L, 1M, 2D, 2L

Row 27> 2L, 2D, 2M, 4L, 1D, 2L, 2ML, 2L, 1M

Row 28< 1ML, 2L, 1D, 1ML, 1M, 2L, 1D, 1L, 1D, 2L, 1M, 1ML, 1D, 2L

Row 29> 1M, 2L, 2ML, 2L, 1D, 4L, 2M, 2D, 2L

Row 30< 1ML, 2L, 2D, 1M, 2L, 1D, 1L, 2D, 2L, 1ML, 2L, 1M

Row 31> 2M, 4L, 5D, 2L, 1M, 1D, 2L, 1ML

Row 32< 2ML, 2L, 1D, 2L, 3D, 1L, 2D, 3L, 2M

Row 33> 1ML, 2M, 2L, 2D, 1L, 1D, 1L, 2D, 4L, 2ML

Row 34< 3ML, 3L, 2D, 1L, 1D, 2L, 2D, 1L, 2M, 1ML

Row 35> 2ML, 2M, 2D, 2L, 1D, 2L, 2D, 2L, 3ML

Row 36< 4ML, 1L, 2D, 2L, 1D, 3L, 1D, 2M, 2ML

Row 37> 3ML, 1M, 1D, 3L, 1D, 3L, 2D, 4ML

Row 38< 4ML, 1M, 1D, 3L, 1D, 1L, 1M, 2L, 1M, 3ML

Row 39> 4ML, 2L, 1M, 1L, 1D, 1L, 1M, 2L, 1M, 4ML

Row 40< 4ML, 1M, 2L, 1M, 1L, 1D, 1L, 2M, 1L, 4ML

Row 41> 4ML, 1L, 1D, 1M, 1L, 1D, 1L, 1M, 1ML, 1L, 1M, 4ML

Row 42< 4ML, 1M, 1L, 1ML, 1M, 1L, 1D, 1L, 1ML, 1D, 1L, 4ML

Row 43> 4ML, 1L, 1D, 1ML, 1L, 1D, 1L, 1M, 1ML, 1L, 1M, 4ML

Row 44< 4ML, 1M, 1L, 1ML, 1D, 1L, 1D, 1L, 1ML, 1D, 1L, 4ML

Row 45> 4ML, 1L, 1D, 1ML, 1L, 1D, 1L, 2D, 1L, 1M, 4ML

Row 46< 4ML, 1M, 1L, 2D, 1L, 1D, 2L, 1D, 1L, 4ML

Row 47> 4ML, 1L, 1D, 2L, 1M, 2L, 1D, 1L, 1M, 4ML

Row 48< 4ML, 1M, 1L, 1D, 2L, 2M, 3L, 4ML

Row 49> 4ML, 3L, 2M, 1ML, 3L, 1M, 4ML

Row 50< 4ML, 1M, 3L, 2ML, 2M, 2L, 4ML

Row 51> 4ML, 2L, 2M, 3ML, 2L, 1M, 4ML

Row 52< 4ML, 1M, 2L, 4ML, 2M, 1L, 4ML

Row 53> 4ML, 1L, 2M, 5ML, 1L, 1M, 4ML

Row 54< 5ML, 1L, 6ML, 2M, 4ML,

Row 55> 5ML, 1M, 12ML

Row 56< 18ML

If you wish to continue with further repeats of the pattern, do Rows 1 & 2 below, then continue with Row 3 above.

Row 1> 12ML, 1M, 1L, 4L

Row 2< 5ML, 1L, 1M, 6ML, 1L, 4ML

<u>Beginning Row (Rows 1 & 2)</u>
1M, 13L, 2M

Row 3> 2M, 5L, 1M

Row 4< 2M, 4L, 2M

Row 5> 1L, 2M, 3L, 2M

Row 6< 1L, 2M, 2L, 2M, 1L

Row 7> 2L, 2M, 1L, 2M, 1L

Row 8< 2L, 4M, 2L

Row 9> 1D, 2L, 1M, 1D, 1M, 2L

Row 10< 1D, 2L, 2D, 2L, 1D

Row 11> 2D, 1L, 3D, 1L, 1D

Row 12< 8D

Row 13> 2D, 1L, 3D, 1L, 1D

Row 14< 1D, 2L, 2D, 2L, 1D

Row 15> 1D, 1M, 2L, 1D, 2L, 1M

Row 16< 2M, 4L, 2M

Row 17> 1L, 2M, 3L, 2M

Row 18< 1L, 2M, 2L, 2M, 1L

Row 19> 2L, 2M, 1L, 2M, 1L

Row 20< 2L, 4M, 2L

Row 21> 3L, 3M, 2L

Row 22< 3L, 2M, 3L

Row 23> 4L, 1M, 4L

Row 24< 8L

If you wish to continue with further repeats of the
pattern, do Rows 1 & 2 below, then continue with
Row 3 above.

Row 1> 1M, 7L

Row 2< 1M, 6L, 1M

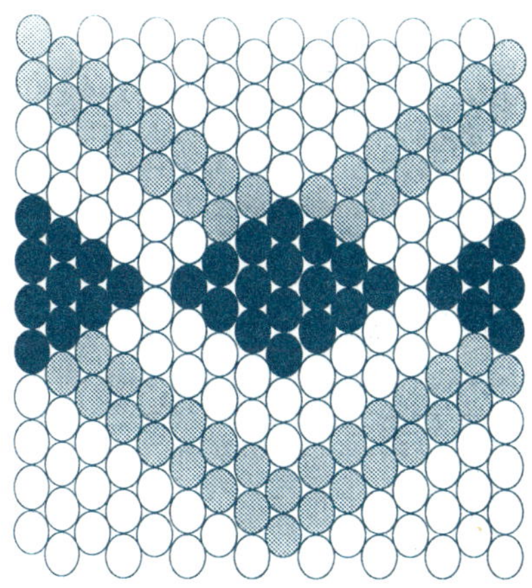

Pattern No. 46
Diamond Waves

Multiple - 16
Repeat - 24 rows

Colors
L = Light
M = Medium
D = Dark

4L, 3D, 3L

Row 3> 1L, 1M, 1D, 1M, 1L

Row 42< 1L, 1M, 2D, 1M

Row 53> 2M, 1D, 2M

Row 6< 1L, 1M, 2L, 1M

Row 75> 1M, 3L, 1M

Row 8< 1L, 1M, 2L, 1M

Row 9> 1M, 3L, 1M

Row 10< 1L, 1M, 2L, 1M

Row 11> 1M, 3L, 1M

Row 12< 1L, 1M, 2L, 1M

Row 13> 2M, 1D, 2M

Row 14< 1L, 1M, 2D, 1M

Row 15> 1L, 1M, 1D, 1M, 1L

Row 16< 2L, 2D, 1L

Row 17> 2L, 1D, 2L

Row 18< 2L, 2D, 1L

If you wish to continue with further repeats of the pattern, do Rows 1 & 2 below, then continue with Row 3 above.

Row 1> 2L, 1D, 2L

Row 2< 2L, 2D, 1L

Pattern No. 47
Bracelet

Multiple - 10
Repeat - 18 rows

Colors
L = Light
M = Medium
D = Dark

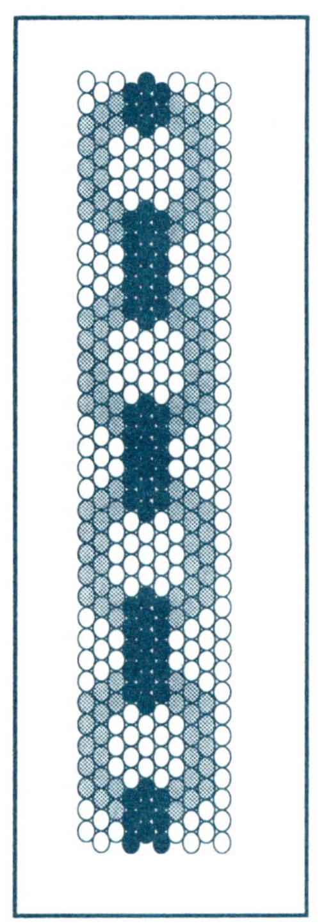

<u>Beginning Row (Rows 1 & 2)</u>
1D, 2M, 1D

Row 3> 1L, 1M

Row 4< 1D, 1L

Row 53> 1D, 1L

Row 6< 1L, 1M

Row 7> 1D, 1M

Row 8< 1D, 1M

Row 9> 1L, 1M

Row 10< 1D, 1L

Row 11> 1D, 1L

Row 12< 1L, 1M

If you wish to continue with further repeats of the pattern, do Rows 1 & 2 below, then continue with Row 3 above.

Row 1> 1D, 1M

Row 2< 1D, 1M

Pattern No. 48
Coil

Multiple - 4
Repeat - 12 rows

Colors
L = Light
M = Medium
D = Dark

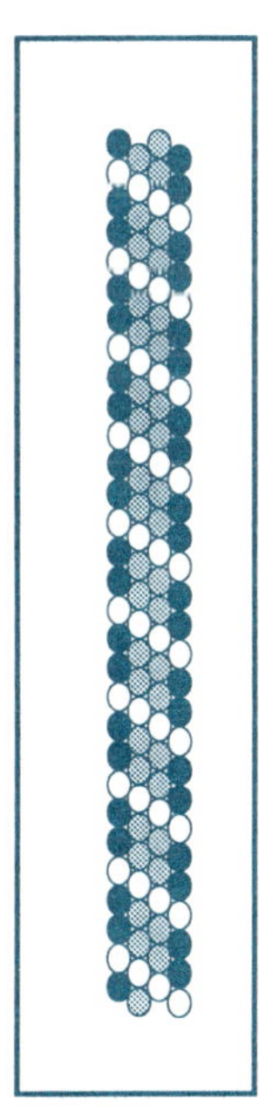

Pattern No. 49
Art Deco 1

Multiple - 22
Repeat - 54 rows

Colors
L = Light
ML = Medium Light
M = Medium
D = Dark

<u>Beginning Row (Rows 1 & 2)</u>
3ML, 2L, 13D, 2L, 2ML

Row 3> 2ML, 1L, 5D, 1L, 2ML

Row 4< 3ML, 1L, 4D, 1L, 2ML

Row 5> 3ML, 1L, 3D, 1L, 3ML

Row 6< 1L, 3ML, 1L, 2D, 1L, 3ML

Row 7> 1L, 3ML, 1L, 1D, 1L, 3ML, 1L

Row 8< 1ML, 1L, 3ML, 2L, 3ML, 1L

Row 9> 1ML, 1L, 3ML, 1L, 3ML, 1L, 1ML

Row 10< 2ML, 1L, 6ML, 1L, 1ML

Row 11> 2ML, 1L, 2ML, 1D, 2ML, 1L, 2ML

Row 12< 3ML, 1L, 1ML, 2D, 1ML, 1L, 2ML

Row 13> 3ML, 1L, 1D, 1ML, 1D, 1L, 3ML

Row 14< 1L, 3ML, 1D, 2ML, 1D, 3ML

Row 15> 1L, 2ML, 1D, 1L, 1ML, 1L, 1D, 2ML, 1L

Row 16< 2L, 1ML, 1D, 1ML, 2L, 1ML, 1D, 1ML, 1L

Row 17> 2L, 1D, 2ML, 1L, 2ML, 1D, 2L

Row 18< 1M, 1L, 1D, 6ML, 1D, 1L

Row 19> 1M, 1D, 1L, 5ML, 1L, 1D, 1M

Row 20< 1L, 1D, 2L, 4ML, 2L, 1D

Row 21> 1D, 1M, 2L, 1ML, 1D, 1ML, 2L, 1M, 1D

Row 22< 1L, 1D, 1M, 2L, 2D, 2L, 1M, 1D

Row 23> 1L, 1D, 1M, 2L, 1D, 2L, 1M, 1D, 1L

Row 24< 3L, 1M, 1L, 2D, 1L, 1M, 2L

Row 25> 1L, 1D, 1L, 1M, 1L, 1D, 1L, 1M, 1L, 1D, 1L

Row 26< 4L, 1M, 2D, 1M, 3L

Row 27> 1L, 1D, 1L, 1M, 1L, 1D, 1L, 1M, 1L, 1D, 1L

Row 28< 3L, 1M, 1L, 2D, 1L, 1M, 2L

Row 29> 1L, 1D, 1M, 2L, 1D, 2L, 1M, 1D, 1L

Row 30< 1L, 1D, 1M, 2L, 2D, 2L, 1M, 1D

Row 31> 1D, 1M, 2L, 1ML, 1D, 1ML, 2L, 1M, 1D

Row 32< 1L, 1D, 2L, 4ML, 2L, 1D

Row 33> 1M, 1D, 1L, 5ML, 1L, 1D, 1M

Row 34< 1M, 1L, 1D, 6ML, 1D, 1L

Row 35> 2L, 1D, 2ML, 1L, 2ML, 1D, 2L

Row 36< 2L, 1ML, 1D, 1ML, 2L, 1ML, 1D, 1ML, 1L

Row 37> 1L, 2ML, 1D, 1L, 1ML, 1L, 1D, 2ML, 1L

Row 38< 1L, 3ML, 1D, 2ML, 1D, 3ML

Row 39> 3ML, 1L, 1D, 1ML, 1D, 1L, 3ML

Row 40< 3ML, 1L, 1ML, 2D, 1ML, 1L, 2ML

Row 41> 2ML, 1L, 2ML, 1D, 2ML, 1L, 2ML

Row 42< 2ML, 1L, 6ML, 1L, 1ML

Row 43> 1ML, 1L, 3ML, 1L, 3ML, 1L, 1ML

Row 44< 1ML, 1L, 3ML, 2L, 3ML, 1L

Row 45> 1L, 3ML, 1L, 1D, 1L, 3ML, 1L

Row 46< 1L, 3ML, 1L, 2D, 1L, 3ML

Row 47> 3ML, 1L, 3D, 1L, 3ML

Row 48< 3ML, 1L, 4D, 1L, 2ML

Row 49> 2ML, 1L, 5D, 1L, 2ML

Row 50< 2ML, 1L, 6D, 1L, 1ML

Row 51> 1ML, 1L, 7D, 1L, 1ML

Row 52< 1ML, 1L, 8D, 1L

Row 53> 1L, 9D, 1L

Row 54< 1ML, 1L, 8D, 1L

If you wish to continue with further repeats of the pattern, do Rows 1 & 2 below, then continue with Row 3 above.

Row 1> 1ML, 1L, 7D, 1L, 1ML

Row 2< 2ML, 1L, 6D, 1L, 1ML

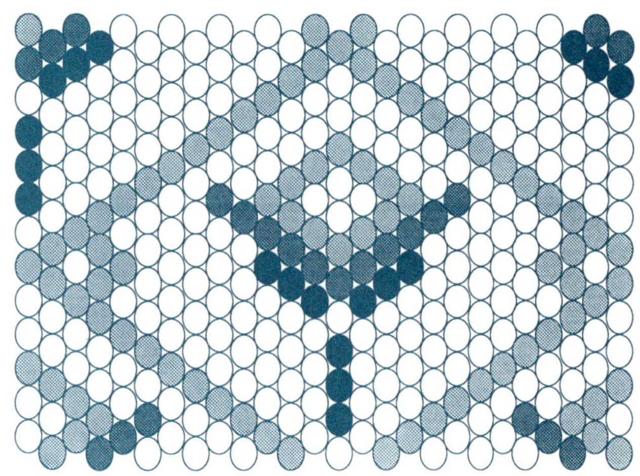

Pattern No. 50
Flower Trellis

Multiple - 26
Repeat - 26 rows

Colors
L = Light
ML = Medium Light
M = Medium
D = Dark

2M, 1D, 8L, 3ML, 8L, 1D, 2M, 1ML

Row 3> 1M, 1D, 4L, 2ML, 4L, 1D

Row 4< 1D, 4L, 1ML, 1L, 1ML, 4L, 1D

Row 5> 5L, 1ML, 2L, 1ML, 4L

Row 6< 4L, 1ML, 3L, 1ML, 4L

Row 7> 1D, 3L, 1ML, 4L, 1ML, 3L

Row 8< 3L, 1ML, 2L, 1ML, 2L, 1ML, 3L

Row 9> 1D, 2L, 1ML, 2L, 2ML, 2L, 1ML, 2L

Row 10< 2L, 1ML, 2L, 1ML, 1L, 1ML, 2L, 1ML, 2L

Row 11> 1D, 1L, 1ML, 1L, 1M, 1ML, 2L, 1ML, 1M, 1L, 1ML, 1L

Row 12< 1L, 1ML, 2L, 1M, 1ML, 1L, 1ML, 1M, 2L, 1ML, 1L

Row 13> 1L, 1ML, 3L, 1M, 2ML, 1M, 3L, 1ML

Row 14< 2ML, 3L, 1M, 1ML, 1M, 3L, 2ML

Row 15> 1ML, 1L, 1ML, 2L, 1D, 2M, 1D, 2L, 1ML, 1L

Row 16< 2ML, 3L, 1D, 1M, 1D, 3L, 2ML

Row 17> 1L, 1ML, 4L, 2D, 4L, 1ML

Row 18< 1L, 1ML, 9L, 1ML, 1L

Row 19> 2L, 1ML, 8L, 1ML, 1L

Row 20< 2L, 1ML, 3L, 1D, 3L, 1ML, 2L

Row 21> 1ML, 2L, 1ML, 6L, 1ML, 2L

Row 22< 1ML, 2L, 1ML, 2L, 1D, 2L, 1ML, 2L, 2ML

Row 23> 1L, 1ML, 2L, 1ML, 4L, 1ML, 2L, 1ML

Row 24< 1L, 1ML, 1M, 1L, 1ML, 1L, 1D, 1L, 1ML, 1L, 1M, 1ML, 1L

Row 25> 1L, 1ML, 1M, 2L, 1ML, 2L, 1ML, 2L, 1M, 1ML

Row 26< 1ML, 1M, 3L, 1ML, 1L, 1ML, 3L, 1M, 1ML

If you wish to continue with further repeats of the pattern, do Rows 1 & 2 below, then continue with Row 3 above.

Row 1> 1ML, 1M, 4L, 2ML, 4L, 1M

Row 2< 1M, 1D, 4L, 1ML, 4L, 1D, 1M

Alphabet

Multiple - 6
Repeat - 12 rows

Colors
L = Light
M = Medium

Bead-Line Graph Paper

Color Key:

Copyright 1994   Diane Fitzgerald
Beautiful Beads, 115 Hennepin Ave.
Minneapolis, MN 55401 - 612-333-0170

Bead-Line Guide

Bead-Line Graph Paper

Color Key:

Beautiful Beads, 115 Hennepin Ave.
Minneapolis, MN 55401 - 612-333-0170

Bead-Line Guide

Bead-Line Graph Paper

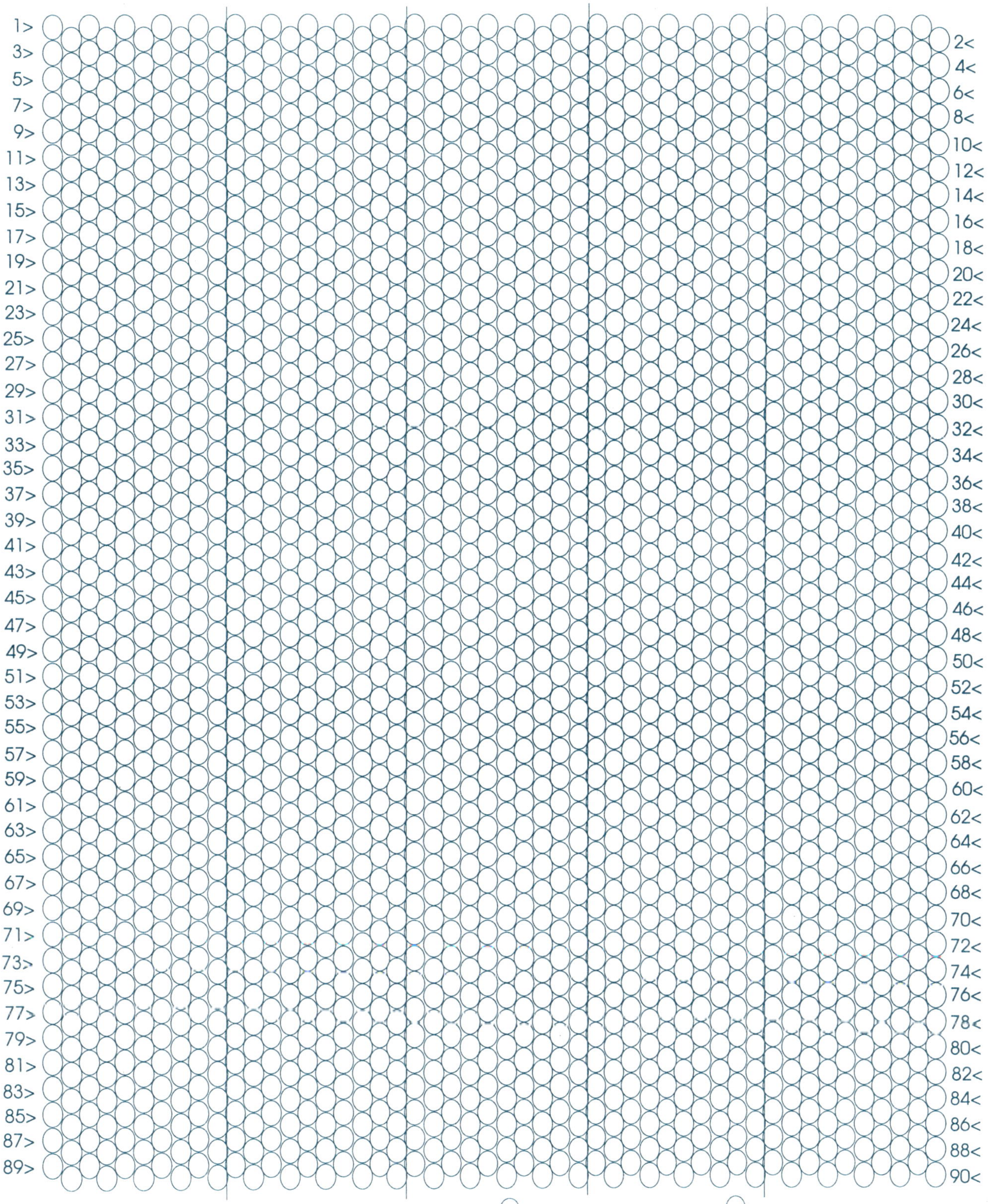

Color Key:

Beautiful Beads, 115 Hennepin Ave.
Minneapolis, MN 55401 - 612-333-0170

Bead-Line Guide

Bead-Line Graph Paper

Color Key:

Copyright 1994   Diane Fitzgerald
Beautiful Beads, 115 Hennepin Ave.
Minneapolis, MN 55401 - 612-333-0170

Bead-Line Guide

Bead-Line Graph Paper

Color Key:

Beautiful Beads, 115 Hennepin Ave.
Minneapolis, MN 55401 - 612-333-0170

Bead-Line Guide